WAR IS A FORCE THAT
GIVES US MEANING

WAR

IS A FORCE THAT
GIVES US MEANING

CHRIS HEDGES

PublicAffairs
NEW YORK

From Homer, *Odyssey*, trans. Stanley Lombardo, copyright © 2000, reprinted by permission of Hackett Publishing Company, Inc. All rights reserved. "Epitaph on a Tyrant", copyright © 1940 & renewed 1968 by W. H. Auden, from *W.H. Auden: The Collected Poems* by W.H. Auden. Used by permission of Random House, Inc. "Wants" from *Collected Poems* by Philip Larkin, copyright © 1988, 1989 by the Estate of Philip Larkin. Reprinted by permission of Farrar, Straus and Giroux, LLC. "Catullus, CI" translated by Robert Fitzgerald, from *In The Rose Of Time*, copyright © 1956 by Robert Fitzgerald. Reprinted by permission of New Directions Publishing Corp. From *Goodbye Darkness* by William Manchester, published by Little, Brown and Company (Back Bay Books), copyright © 1979, 1980 by William Manchester. Reprinted by permission of Don Congdon Associates, Inc.

LIBRARY OF CONGRESS CATALOGING-IN-PUBLICATION DATA

Hedges, Chris.

War is a force that gives us meaning / Chris Hedges.—1st ed.

p. cm.

Includes index.

ISBN 1-58648-049-9

1. War (Philosophy) 2. Hedges, Chris. 3. Military history, Modern—20th century. I. Title.

U21.2 .H43 2002

355.02—dc21

2002068136

3 5 7 9 10 8 6 4 2

For my father, the Rev. Thomas Hedges,

who taught me that compassion was the highest virtue,

and for the Rev. Coleman Brown,

who has never let me forget it.

CONTENTS

If in smothering dreams you too could pace
Behind the wagon that we flung him in,
And watch the white eyes writhing in his face,
His hanging face, like a devil's sick of sin;
If you could hear, at every jolt, the blood
Come gargling from the froth-corrupted lungs,
Obscene as cancer, bitter as the cud
Of vile, incurable sores on innocent tongues, —
My friend, you would not tell with such high zest
To children ardent for some desperate glory,
The old Lie: Dulce et decorum est
Pro Patria mori.

·

WILFRED OWEN
Dulce et decorum est

WAR IS A FORCE THAT
GIVES US MEANING

INTRODUCTION

Only the dead have seen the end of war.

•

PLATO

SARAJEVO IN THE SUMMER OF 1995 CAME CLOSE TO
Dante's inner circle of hell. The city, surrounded by Serb
gunners on the heights above, was subjected to hundreds of
shells a day, all crashing into an area twice the size of Central
Park. Ninety-millimeter tank rounds and blasts fired from huge
155-millimeter howitzers set up a deadly rhythm of detonations.
Multiple Katyusha rockets—whooshing overhead—burst in
rapid succession; they could take down a four- or five-story
apartment building in seconds, killing or wounding everyone
inside. There was no running water or electricity and little to eat;
most people were subsisting on a bowl of soup a day. It was
possible to enter the besieged city only by driving down a dirt
track on Mount Igman, one stretch directly in the line of Serb
fire. The vehicles that had failed to make it lay twisted and
upended in the ravine below, at times with the charred remains
of their human cargo inside.

Families lived huddled in basements, and mothers, who had
to make a mad dash to the common water taps set up by the
United Nations, faced an excruciating choice—whether to run
through the streets with their children or leave them in a building that might be rubble when they returned.

The hurling bits of iron fragmentation from exploding shells left bodies mangled, dismembered, decapitated. The other reporters and I slipped and slid in the blood and entrails thrown out by the shell blasts, heard the groans of anguish, and were, for our pains, in the sights of Serb snipers, often just a few hundred yards away. The latest victims lay with gaping wounds untended in the corridors of the hospitals that lacked antibiotics and painkillers.

When the cease-fires broke down, there would be four to five dead a day, and a dozen wounded. It was a roulette wheel of death, a wheel of fire that knew no distinctions of rank or nationality. By that summer, after nearly four years of fighting, forty-five foreign reporters had been killed, scores wounded. I lived—sheltered in a side room in the Holiday Inn, its front smashed and battered by shellfire—in a world bent on self-destruction, a world where lives were snuffed out at random.

War and conflict have marked most of my adult life. I began covering insurgencies in El Salvador, where I spent five years, then went on to Guatemala and Nicaragua and Colombia, through the first *intifada* in the West Bank and Gaza, the civil war in the Sudan and Yemen, the uprisings in Algeria and the Punjab, the fall of the Romanian dictator Nicolae Ceauşescu, the Gulf War, the Kurdish rebellion in southeast Turkey and northern Iraq, the war in Bosnia, and finally to Kosovo. I have been in ambushes on desolate stretches of Central American roads, shot at in the marshes of southern Iraq, imprisoned in the Sudan, beaten by Saudi military police, deported from Libya and Iran, captured and held for a week by Iraqi Republican Guard during the Shiite rebellion following the Gulf War, strafed by Russian Mig–21s in Bosnia, fired upon by Serb snipers, and shelled for days in Sarajevo with deafening rounds of heavy artillery that threw out thousands of deadly bits of iron fragments. I have seen too much of violent death. I have tasted too much of my own fear. I have painful memories that lie buried and untouched most of the time. It is never easy when they surface.

I learned early on that war forms its own culture. The rush of battle is a potent and often lethal addiction, for war is a drug, one I ingested for many years. It is peddled by mythmakers— historians, war correspondents, filmmakers, novelists, and the state—all of whom endow it with qualities it often does possess: excitement, exoticism, power, chances to rise above our small stations in life, and a bizarre and fantastic universe that has a grotesque and dark beauty. It dominates culture, distorts memory, corrupts language, and infects everything around it, even humor, which becomes preoccupied with the grim perversities of smut and death. Fundamental questions about the meaning, or meaninglessness, of our place on the planet are laid bare when we watch those around us sink to the lowest depths. War exposes the capacity for evil that lurks not far below the surface within all of us. And this is why for many war is so hard to discuss once it is over.

The enduring attraction of war is this: Even with its destruction and carnage it can give us what we long for in life. It can give us purpose, meaning, a reason for living. Only when we are in the midst of conflict does the shallowness and vapidness of much of our lives become apparent. Trivia dominates our conversations and increasingly our airwaves. And war is an enticing elixir. It gives us resolve, a cause. It allows us to be noble. And those who have the least meaning in their lives, the impoverished refugees in Gaza, the disenfranchised North African immigrants in France, even the legions of young who live in the splendid indolence and safety of the industrialized world, are all susceptible to war's appeal.

Those who make war do so for many reasons, although many of these motives are never acknowledged publicly.

The Palestinian uprising was not just about throwing the Israelis out of Gaza and the West Bank, but also about crushing the urban elite, the shop owners and businessmen, in East Jerusalem and Gaza City. The "strikes" organized by the *shabab*, the young men who fueled the uprising from the refugee camps, hurt the Palestinian community far more than they hurt the Israelis. In Bosnia it was the same, the anger turned against a Communist hierarchy that kept for itself the privileges and perks of power even as power slipped from their hands in the decaying state. There is little that angers the disenfranchised more than those who fail to exercise power yet reap powerful rewards. Despots can be understood, even tolerated, but parasites rarely last long.

War is a crusade. President George W. Bush is not shy about warning other nations that they stand with the United States in the war on terrorism or will be counted with those that defy us. This too is a *jihad*. Yet we Americans find ourselves in the dangerous position of going to war not against a state but against a phantom. The *jihad* we have embarked upon is targeting an elusive and protean enemy. The battle we have begun is neverending. But it may be too late to wind back the heady rhetoric. We have embarked on a campaign as quixotic as the one mounted to destroy us.

"We go forward," President Bush assures us, "to defend freedom and all that is good and just in the world."

The patriotic bunting and American flags that proliferated in the wake of the attacks on the World Trade Center and the Pentagon were our support for the war mounted against the "axis of evil." Elected officials, celebrities and news anchors lined up to be counted. On Friday, September 14, three days after the attacks, Congress granted the President the right to "use all necessary and appropriate force against those nations, organizations, or persons he determines planned, authorized, committed, or aided the terrorist attacks." The resolution was passed unanimously by the Senate. There was in the House only one dissenting vote, from Barbara J. Lee, a Democrat from California, who warned that military action could not guarantee the safety of the country and that "as we act, let us not become the evil we deplore."

When we ingest the anodyne of war we feel what those we strive to destroy feel, including the Islamic fundamentalists who are painted as alien, barbaric, and uncivilized. It is the same narcotic. I partook of it for many years. And like every recovering addict there is a part of me that remains nostalgic for war's simplicity and high, even as I cope with the scars it has left behind, mourn the deaths of those I worked with, and struggle with the bestiality I would have been better off not witnessing. There is a part of me—maybe it is a part of many of us—that decided at certain moments that I would rather die like this than go back to the routine of life. The chance to exist for an intense and overpowering moment, even if it meant certain oblivion, seemed worth it in the midst of war—and very stupid once the war ended.

I covered the war in El Salvador from 1983 to 1988. By the end I had a nervous twitch in my face. I was evacuated three times by the U.S. embassy because of tips that the death squads planned to kill me. Yet each time I came back. I accepted with a grim fatalism that I would be killed in El Salvador. I could not articulate why I should accept my own destruction and cannot now. When I finally did leave, my last act was, in a frenzy of rage and anguish, to leap over the KLM counter in the airport in Costa Rica because of a perceived slight by a hapless airline clerk. I beat him to the floor as his bewildered colleagues locked themselves in the room behind the counter. Blood streamed down his face and mine. I refused to wipe the dried stains off my cheeks on the flight to Madrid, and I carry a scar on my face from where he thrust his pen into my cheek. War's sickness had become mine.

In the fall of 1995, a few weeks after the war in Bosnia ended, I sat with friends who had suffered horribly. A young woman, Ljiljana, had lost her father, a Serb who refused to join the besieging Serb forces around the city. She had been forced a few days earlier to identify his corpse. The body was lifted, the water running out of the sides of a rotting coffin, from a small park for reburial in the central cemetery. She was emigrating to Australia soon—where, she told me, "I will marry a man who has never heard of this war and raise children who will be told nothing about it, nothing about the country I am from."

Ljiljana was beautiful and young, but the war had exacted a toll. Her cheeks were hollow, her hair dry and brittle. Her teeth were decayed and some had broken into jagged bits. She had no money for a dentist. She hoped to fix them in Australia.

Yet all she and her friends did that afternoon was lament the days when they lived in fear and hunger, emaciated, targeted by Serbian gunners on the heights above. They did not wish back the suffering, and yet, they admitted, those days may have been the fullest of their lives. They looked at me in despair. I knew them when they were being stonked by hundreds of shells a day, when they had no water to bathe in or to wash their clothes, when they huddled in unheated, darkened apartments with plastic sheeting for windows. But what they expressed was real. It was the disillusionment with a sterile, futile, empty present. Peace had again exposed the void that the rush of war, of battle, had filled. Once again they were, as perhaps we all are, alone, no longer bound by that common sense of struggle, no longer given the opportunity to be noble, heroic, no longer sure what life was about or what it meant.

The old comradeship, however false, that allowed them to love men and women they hardly knew, indeed, whom they may not have liked before the war, had vanished. Moreover, they had seen that all the sacrifice had been for naught. They had been betrayed. The corrupt old Communist Party bosses, who became nationalists overnight and got my friends into the mess in the first place, those who had grown rich off their suffering, were still in power. There was a 70 percent unemployment rate. They depended on handouts from the international community. They knew the lie of war, the mockery of their idealism and struggled with their shattered illusions. They had seen the grinning skull of death that speaks in the end for war. They understood that their cause, once as fashionable in certain intellectual circles as they were themselves, lay forgotten. No longer did actors, politicians, and artists scramble to visit, acts that were almost always ones of gross self-promotion. And yet they wished it all back. I did too.

A year later I received a Christmas card. It was signed "Ljiljana from Australia." It had no return address. I never heard from her again.

Many of us, restless and unfulfilled, see no supreme worth in our lives. We want more out of life. And war, at least, gives a sense that we can rise above our smallness and divisiveness.

The weeks after the September 11 attacks saw New York City, with some reluctance, slip back to normal. One felt the same nostalgia.

The attacks on the World Trade Center illustrate that those who oppose us, rather than coming from another moral universe, have been schooled well in modern warfare. The dramatic explosions, the fireballs, the victims plummeting to their deaths, the collapse of the towers in Manhattan, were straight out of Hollywood. Where else, but from the industrialized world, did the suicide hijackers learn that huge explosions and death above a city skyline are a peculiar and effective form of communication? They have mastered the language. They understand that the use of disproportionate violence against innocents is a way to make a statement. We leave the same calling cards.

Corpses in wartime often deliver messages. The death squads in El Salvador dumped three bodies in the parking lot of the Camino Real Hotel in San Salvador, where the journalists were based, early one morning. Death threats against us were stuffed in the mouths of the bodies. And, on a larger scale, Washington uses murder and corpses to transmit its wrath. We delivered such incendiary messages in Vietnam, Iraq, Serbia, and Afghanistan. Osama bin Laden has learned to speak the language of modern industrial warfare. It was Robert McNamara, the American Secretary of Defense in the summer of 1965, who defined the bombing raids that would eventually leave hundreds of thousands of civilians north of Saigon dead as a means of communication to the Communist regime in Hanoi.

It is part of war's perversity that we lionize those who make great warriors and excuse their excesses in the name of self-defense. We have built or bolstered alliances with Israel and

Russia, forming a dubious global troika against terrorism, a troika that taints us in the eyes of much of the rest of the world, especially among Muslims. Suddenly all who oppose our allies and us—Palestinians, Chechens, and Afghans—are lumped into one indistinguishable mass. They are as faceless as we are for our enemies.

As the battle against terrorism continues, as terrorist attacks intrude on our lives, as we feel less and less secure, the acceptance of all methods to lash out at real and perceived enemies will distort and deform our democracy. For even as war gives meaning to sterile lives, it also promotes killers and racists.

Organized killing is done best by a disciplined, professional army. But war also empowers those with a predilection for murder. Petty gangsters, reviled in pre-war Sarajevo, were transformed overnight at the start of the conflict into war heroes. What they did was no different. They still pillaged, looted, tortured, raped, and killed; only then they did it to Serbs, and with an ideological veneer. Slobodan Milošević went one further. He opened up the country's prisons and armed his criminal class to fight in Bosnia. Once we sign on for war's crusade, once we see ourselves on the side of the angels, once we embrace a theological or ideological belief system that defines itself as the embodiment of goodness and light, it is only a matter of how we will carry out murder.

The eruption of conflict instantly reduces the headache and trivia of daily life. The communal march against an enemy generates a warm, unfamiliar bond with our neighbors, our community, our nation, wiping out unsettling undercurrents of alienation and dislocation. War, in times of malaise and desperation, is a potent distraction.

George Orwell in *1984* wrote of the necessity of constant

wars against the Other to forge a false unity among the proles: "War had been literally continuous, though strictly speaking it had not always been the same war.... The enemy of the moment always represented absolute evil."[1]

Patriotism, often a thinly veiled form of collective self-worship, celebrates our goodness, our ideals, our mercy and bemoans the perfidiousness of those who hate us. Never mind the murder and repression done in our name by bloody surrogates from the Shah of Iran to the Congolese dictator Joseph-Désiré Mobutu, who received from Washington well over a billion dollars in civilian and military aid during the three decades of his rule. And European states—especially France—gave Mobutu even more as he bled dry one of the richest countries in Africa. We define ourselves. All other definitions do not count.

War makes the world understandable, a black and white tableau of them and us. It suspends thought, especially self-critical thought. All bow before the supreme effort. We are one. Most of us willingly accept war as long as we can fold it into a belief system that paints the ensuing suffering as necessary for a higher good, for human beings seek not only happiness but also meaning. And tragically war is sometimes the most powerful way in human society to achieve meaning.

But war is a god, as the ancient Greeks and Romans knew, and its worship demands human sacrifice. We urge young men to war, making the slaughter they are asked to carry out a rite of passage. And this rite has changed little over the centuries, centuries in which there has almost continuously been a war raging somewhere on the planet. The historian Will Durant calculated that there have only been twenty-nine years in all of human history during which a war was not underway somewhere. We call on the warrior to exemplify the qualities necessary to prosecute war—courage, loyalty, and self-sacrifice. The soldier, neglected and even shunned during peacetime, is suddenly held up as the exemplar of our highest ideals, the savior of the state. The soldier is often whom we want to become, although secretly many of us, including most soldiers, know that we can never match the ideal held out before us. And we all become like Nestor in *The Iliad*, reciting the litany of fallen heroes that went before to spur on a new generation. That the myths are lies, that those who went before us were no more able to match the ideal than we are, is carefully hidden from public view. The tension between those who know combat, and thus know the public lie, and those who propagate the myth, usually ends with the mythmakers working to silence the witnesses of war.

John Wheeler, who graduated from West Point in 1966, went to Vietnam, where he watched his class take the highest number of dead and wounded of all the classes that fought there. "I was a witness in Vietnam," he told me. "I spent half my time in a helicopter traveling around the country. I was a witness to the decimation of my West Point class. And I knew we were decimated for a lie." He left the army as a captain in 1971, went to Yale Law School, and became an activist. He was the driving force behind the Vietnam Veterans Memorial wall in Washington. "When I left law school the full impact of the lies hit me," he said. "I have been thinking about these lies, meditating on them and acting on them ever since. The honor system at West Point failed grotesquely within the chain of command. The most senior officers went along with McNamara and Johnson and were guilty. It was an abomination. If in order to do your duty as an Admiral or a General you have to lie, West Point should tell the new plebes."

The Iliad is about power and force. Those who inhabit its space abide by the warrior's code. Its heroes are vain, brave, and consumed by the heady elixir of violence and the bitterness of bereavement. The story is primarily that of one man, Achilles, who returns to the battlefield at Troy to attain *kleos*, the everlasting fame that will be denied to him without heroic death. *The Iliad* could have been written about Bosnia, with its competing warlords and its commanders willing to sacrifice men and villages to their egos and ambition.

The Odyssey is different. It is also built around one character, Odysseus. In *The Odyssey* the hubris and inflexibility of the warrior fail to ward off the capriciousness of fate, the indifference of nature. Odysseus has trouble coping with the conventions of civilized life. When he takes umbrage at more powerful forces and cannot resist revealing his name to the Cyclops, he condemns his men to death and himself to prolonged suffering. As the sailors beat the sea to white froth with their oars, Odysseus calls out to Cyclops: "With my men / hanging all over me and begging me not to," but they "didn't persuade my hero's heart."[2]

It is his hero's heart that Odysseus must learn to curb before he can return to the domestic life he left twenty years earlier. The very qualities that served him in battle defeat him in peace. These dual codes have existed, perhaps, since human societies were formed, and every recruit headed into war would be well-advised to read *The Iliad*, just as every soldier returning home would be served by reading *The Odyssey*. No two works have come closer to chronicling the rage and consumption of war and the struggle to recover. The name Odysseus is tied to the Greek verb *odussomai*, which means "to suffer pain."

War exposes a side of human nature that is usually masked by the unacknowledged coercion and social constraints that glue us together. Our cultivated conventions and little lies of civility lull us into a refined and idealistic view of ourselves. But modern industrial warfare may well be leading us, with each technological advance, a step closer to our own annihilation. We too are strapping explosives around our waists. Do we also have a suicide pact?

Look just at the 1990s: 2 million dead in Afghanistan; 1.5 million dead in the Sudan; some 800,000 butchered in ninety days in Rwanda; a half-million dead in Angola; a quarter of a million dead in Bosnia; 200,000 dead in Guatemala; 150,000 dead in Liberia; a quarter of a million dead in Burundi; 75,000 dead in Algeria; and untold tens of thousands lost in the border conflict between Ethiopia and Eritrea, the fighting in Columbia, the Israeli-Palestinian conflict, Chechnya, Sri Lanka, southeastern Turkey, Sierra Leone, Northern Ireland, Kosovo, and the Persian Gulf War (where perhaps as many as 35,000 Iraqi citizens were killed). In the wars of the twentieth century not less than 62 million civilians have perished, nearly 20 million more than the 43 million military personnel killed.

Civil war, brutality, ideological intolerance, conspiracy, and murderous repression are part of the human condition—indeed almost the daily fare for many but a privileged minority.

War is not a uniform experience or event. My time in the insurgencies in Central America, the Persian Gulf War—where two large armies clashed in the desert—and the Balkans, where warlords and gangsters tried to pass themselves off as professional soldiers, illustrated the wide differences that make up modern warfare. But war usually demands, by its very logic, the disabling of the enemy, often broadly defined to include civilians who may have little love for the Taliban or Saddam Hussein or Somali warlords. While we venerate and mourn our own dead we are curiously indifferent about those we kill. Thus killing is done in our name, killing that concerns us little, while those who kill our own are seen as having crawled out of the deepest recesses of the earth, lacking our own humanity and goodness. Our dead. Their dead. They are not the same. Our dead matter, theirs do not. Many Israelis defend the killing of Palestinian children whose only crime was to throw rocks at armored patrols, while many Palestinians applaud the murder of Israeli children by suicide bombers.

Armed movements seek divine sanction and the messianic certitude of absolute truth. They do not need to get this from religions, as we usually think of religion, but a type of religion: Patriotism provides the blessing. Soldiers want at least the consolation of knowing that they risk being blown up by land mines for a greater glory, for a New World. Dissension, questioning of purpose, the exposure of war crimes carried out by those fighting on our behalf are dangerous to such beliefs. Dissidents who challenge the goodness of our cause, who question the gods of war, who pull back the curtains to expose the lie are usually silenced or ignored.

We speak of those we fight only in the abstract; we strip them of their human qualities. It is a familiar linguistic corruption. During the war in Bosnia, many Muslims called the Serbs "Chetniks," the Serbian irregulars in World War II, who slaughtered many Muslims. Muslims, for many Serbs in Bosnia, were painted as Islamic fundamentalists. The Croats, to the Serbs and Muslims, were branded "Ustashe," the fascist quislings who ruled Croatia during World War II. And there were times when, in interviews, it was hard to know if people were talking about what happened a few months ago or a few decades ago. It all merged into one huge mythic campaign. It was as if Josip Broz

Tito, who had held Yugoslavia together for most of the Cold War era, had put the conflicted country into a deep freeze in 1945.

The goal of such nationalist rhetoric is to invoke pity for one's own. The goal is to show the community that what they hold sacred is under threat. The enemy, we are told, seeks to destroy religious and cultural life, the very identity of the group or state. Nationalist songs, epic poems, twisted accounts of history take the place of scholarship and art.

America is not immune. We mourn the victims of the World Trade Center attack. Their pictures cover subway walls. We mourn the firefighters, as well we should. But we are blind to those whom we and our allies in the Middle East have crushed or whose rights have been ignored for decades. They seem not to count.

"The principle of the movement is whoever is not included is excluded, whoever is not with me is against me, so the world loses all the nuances and pluralistic aspects that have become too confusing for the masses," wrote Hannah Arendt in *The Origins of Totalitarianism*.[3]

Before conflicts begin, the first people silenced—often with violence—are not the nationalist leaders of the opposing ethnic or religious group, who are useful in that they serve to dump gasoline on the evolving conflict. Those voices within the ethnic group or the nation that question the state's lust and need for war are targeted. These dissidents are the most dangerous. They give us an alternative language, one that refuses to define the other as "barbarian" or "evil," one that recognizes the humanity of the enemy, one that does not condone violence as a form of communication. Such voices are rarely heeded. And until we learn once again to speak in our own voice and reject that handed to us by the state in times of war, we flirt with our own destruction.

And yet, despite all this, I am not a pacifist. I respect and admire the qualities of professional soldiers. Without the determination and leadership of soldiers like General Wesley K. Clark we might not have intervened in Kosovo or Bosnia. It was, in the end, a general, Ulysses S. Grant who saved the union. Even as I detest the pestilence that is war and fear its deadly addiction, even as I see it lead states and groups towards self-immolation, even as I concede that it is war that has left millions of dead and maimed across the planet, I, like most reporters in Sarajevo and Kosovo, desperately hoped for armed intervention. The poison that is war does not free us from the ethics of responsibility. There are times when we must take this poison—just as a person with cancer accepts chemotherapy to live. We can not succumb to despair. Force is and I suspect always will be part of the human condition. There are times when the force wielded by one immoral faction must be countered by a faction that, while never moral, is perhaps less immoral.

We in the industrialized world bear responsibility for the world's genocides because we had the power to intervene and did not. We stood by and watched the slaughter in Chechnya, Sri Lanka, Sierra Leone, Liberia, and Rwanda where a million people died. The blood of the victims of Srebrenica—a designated U.N. safe area in Bosnia—is on our hands. The generation before mine watched, with much the same passivity, the genocides of Germany, Poland, Hungary, Greece, and the Ukraine. These slaughters were, as in Gabriel García Márquez's book *Chronicle of a Death Foretold*, often announced in advance.[4] Hutu radio broadcasts from Kigali called on the Interahamwe in Rwanda to carry out genocide. The U.N. Belgian detachment, however, like the Dutch peacekeepers in Srebrenica, stood by and watched. The radio in Kigali was never shut down. The rampages began. There was never any secret about Milošević's plans for a greater Serbia or his intent to use force and ethnic cleansing to create it.

I wrote this book not to dissuade us from war but to understand it. It is especially important that we, who wield such massive force across the globe, see within ourselves the seeds of our own obliteration. We must guard against the myth of war and the drug of war that can, together, render us as blind and callous as some of those we battle.

We were humbled in Vietnam, purged, for a while, of a dangerous hubris, offered in our understanding and reflection about the war, a moment of grace. We became a better country. But once again the message is slipping away from us, even as we confront the possibility of devastating biological or nuclear terrorist attacks in Washington or New York. If the humility we gained from our defeat in Vietnam is not the engine that drives our response to future terrorist strikes, even those that are cataclysmic, we are lost.

The only antidote to ward off self-destruction and the indiscriminate use of force is humility and, ultimately, compassion. Reinhold Niebuhr aptly reminded us that we must all act and then ask for forgiveness. This book is not a call for inaction. It is a call for repentance.

1

THE MYTH OF WAR

When our own nation is at war with any other, we detest them under the character of cruel, perfidious, unjust and violent: But always esteem ourselves and allies equitable, moderate, and merciful. If the general of our enemies be successful, 'tis with difficulty we allow him the figure and character of a man. He is a sorcerer: He has a communication with daemons; as is reported of Oliver Cromwell, and the Duke of Luxembourg: He is bloody-minded, and takes a pleasure in death and destruction. But if the success be on our side, our commander has all the opposite good qualities, and is a pattern of virtue, as well as of courage and conduct. His treachery we call policy: His cruelty is an evil inseparable from war. In short, every one of his faults we either endeavour to extenuate, or dignify it with the name of that virtue, which approaches it. It is evident the same method of thinking runs thro' common life.

•

DAVID HUME
A Treatise on Human Nature, 1740

THE ETHNIC CONFLICTS AND INSURGENCIES OF OUR TIME,
whether between Serbs and Muslims or Hutus and Tutsis,
are not religious wars. They are not clashes between cultures or
civilizations, nor are they the result of ancient ethnic hatreds.
They are manufactured wars, born out of the collapse of civil
societies, perpetuated by fear, greed, and paranoia, and they are
run by gangsters, who rise up from the bottom of their own
societies and terrorize all, including those they purport to
protect.

Often, none of this is apparent from the outside. We are
quick to accept the facile and mendacious ideological veneer
that is wrapped like a mantle around the shoulders of those
who prosecute the war. In part we do this to avoid intervention,
to give this kind of slaughter an historical inevitability it does
not have, but also because the media and most of the politicians
often lack the perspective and analysis to debunk the myths
served up by the opposing sides.

The United States and the West based our responses in
Bosnia, or perhaps it is better to say our arguments not to
respond, on such myths: the myth of the Serbian warrior who
would fight to the death against overwhelming odds; the myth
that the Croats, Muslims, and Serbs, who speak the same language and are nearly indistinguishable, were different people;
the myth that Yugoslavia, a country that Josip Broz Tito made
an important player in international affairs, had failed to give its
citizens a national identity. These myths, swallowed whole, permitted us to stand by as 250,000 human beings were killed and
Sarajevo spent three and a half years under siege. Although the
United States finally intervened, we did so because the United
Nations mission collapsed in the summer of 1995, not because
of any foresight or courage on the part of the administration of
President Bill Clinton.

Look not to religion and mythology and warped versions of history to find the roots of these conflicts, but to the warlords who dominated the Balkans. It took Milošević four years of hate propaganda and lies, pumped forth daily over the airways from Belgrade, before he got one Serb to cross the border into Bosnia and begin the murderous rampage that triggered the war. And although the war was painted from afar as a clash of rival civilizations, the primary task of Milošević in Serbia, Franjo Tudjman in Croatia, and the other ethnic leaderships was to dismantle and silence their own intellectuals and writers of stature and replace them with second-rate, mediocre pawns willing to turn every intellectual and artistic endeavor into a piece of ethnic triumphalism and myth.

Lawrence LeShan in *The Psychology of War* differentiates between "mythic reality" and "sensory reality" in wartime.[1] In sensory reality we see events for what they are. Most of those who are thrust into combat soon find it impossible to maintain the mythic perception of war. They would not survive if they did. Wars that lose their mythic stature for the public, such as Korea or Vietnam, are doomed to failure, for war is exposed for what it is—organized murder.

But in mythic war we imbue events with meanings they do not have. We see defeats as signposts on the road to ultimate victory. We demonize the enemy so that our opponent is no longer human. We view ourselves, our people, as the embodiment of absolute goodness. Our enemies invert our view of the world to justify their own cruelty. In most mythic wars this is the case. Each side reduces the other to objects—eventually in the form of corpses.

"Force," Simone Weil wrote, "is as pitiless to the man who possesses it, or thinks he does, as it is to its victims; the second it crushes, the first it intoxicates."[2]

When we allow mythic reality to rule, as it almost always does in war, then there is only one solution—force. In mythic war we fight absolutes. We must vanquish darkness. It is imperative and inevitable for civilization, for the free world, that good triumph, just as Islamic militants see us as infidels whose existence corrupts the pure Islamic society they hope to build.

But the goal we seek when we embrace myth is impossible to achieve. War never creates the security or the harmony we desire, especially the harmony we briefly attain during wartime. And campaigns, such as the one in Afghanistan, become starting points for further conflicts, especially as we find that we are unable to root out terrorism or maintain the kind of solidarity that comes in the days just after a terrorist attack.

The chief institutions that disseminate the myth are the press and the state. The press has been culpable since the telegraph made possible the modern war correspondent. And starting with the Crimean War, when the first dispatches were fed by newly minted war correspondents in real time, nearly every reporter has seen his or her mission as sustaining civilian and army morale. The advent of photography and film did little to alter the incentive to boost morale, for the lie in war is almost always the lie of omission. The blunders and senseless slaughter by our generals, the execution of prisoners and innocents, and the horror of wounds are rarely disclosed, at least during a mythic war, to the public. Only when the myth is punctured, as it eventually was in Vietnam, does the press begin to report in a sensory rather than a mythic manner. But even then it is it reacting to a public that has changed its perception of war. The press usually does not lead.

Mythic war reporting sells papers and boosts ratings. Real reporting, sensory reporting, does not, at least not in comparison with the boosterism we witnessed during the Persian Gulf War and the war in Afghanistan. The coverage in the Persian Gulf War was typical. The international press willingly administered a restrictive pool system on behalf of the military under which carefully controlled groups of reporters were guided around the front lines by officers. It could have never functioned without the cooperation of the press. The press was as eager to be of service to the state during the war as most everyone else.

Such docility on the part of the press made it easier to do what governments do in wartime, indeed what governments do much of the time, and that is lie. When Iraqi troops seized the Saudi border town of Khafji, sending Saudi troops fleeing in panic, the headlong retreat was never mentioned. Two French photographers and I watched as frantic Saudi soldiers raced away from the fighting, dozens crowded on a fire truck that tore down the road. U.S. Marines were called in to push the Iraqis back. We stood on rooftops with young Marine radio operators who called in air strikes as Marine units battled Iraqi troops in the streets.

Yet back in Riyadh and Dhahran military press officers spoke about our Saudi allies defending their homeland.

The potency of myth is that it allows us to make sense of mayhem and violent death. It gives a justification to what is often nothing more than gross human cruelty and stupidity. It allows us to believe we have achieved our place in human society because of a long chain of heroic endeavors, rather than accept the sad reality that we stumble along a dimly lit corridor of disasters. It disguises our powerlessness. It hides from view our own impotence and the ordinariness of our own leaders. By turning history into myth we transform random events into a chain of events directed by a will greater than our own, one that is determined and preordained. We are elevated above the multitude. We march toward nobility. And no society is immune.

Most national myths, at their core, are racist. They are fed by ignorance. Those individuals who understand other cultures, speak other languages, and find richness in diversity are shunted aside. Science, history, and psychology are often twisted to serve myth. And many intellectuals are willing to champion and defend absurd theories for nationalist ends.

By finding our identity and meaning in separateness the myth serves another important function: It makes communication with our opponents impossible. When the Palestinian leader Yasir Arafat makes statements that call for moderation and peace he is accused by the Israelis of using words to conceal his intention to wipe out Israel. The Palestinians react in the same manner to statements by most Israeli leaders. It does not matter what they say, just as it did not matter what the Serb or Croat nationalists said to each other; the intentions of the other were predetermined by nationalist myth.

We often become as deaf and dumb as those we condemn. We too have our terrorists. The Contras in Nicaragua carried out, with funding from Washington, some of the most egregious human rights violations in Central America, yet were lauded as "freedom fighters." Jonas Savimbi, the rebel leader the United States backed in Angola's civil war, murdered and tortured with a barbarity that far outstripped the Taliban. The rebellion Savimbi began in 1975 resulted in more than 500,000 dead. President Ronald Reagan called Savimbi the Abraham Lincoln of Angola, although he littered the country with land mines, once bombed a Red Cross–run factory making artificial legs for victims of those mines, and pummeled a rival's wife and children to death. The mayhem and blood-letting we backed in Angola were copied in many parts of Africa, including Zaire and Liberia.

The myth of war sells and legitimizes the drug of war. Once we begin to take war's heady narcotic, it creates an addiction that slowly lowers us to the moral depravity of all addicts. War's utter depravity was captured in Shakespeare's play *Troilus and Cressida*, a work that as far as is known was never performed in Shakespeare's lifetime, perhaps due to its savage indictment of war and human society. Nearly every figure in the play, including Ulysses, lies to and tries to manipulate those around him: that is the trait of most leaders, no matter what political agenda they espouse. Here, unlike *Henry V*, Shakespeare excoriates the established order; the play is one that debunks national myth. There are only three characters who speak about war with any sanity or truth: Pandarus, who is a lecher and a coward; Cassandra, who is deranged; and Thersites, as described by Shakespeare, "a deformed and scurrilous Greek."[3] Yet Thersites' bleak view of human nature and human folly is borne out by the play's end. We are left with the realization that characters who are, by the standards of civil society, the most retrograde stand above the baseness of those who prosecute war, if only because they speak the truth.

"Lechery, lechery, still wars and lechery, nothing else holds fashion," Thersites rails.[4]

War can be the natural outcome of brutal repression; witness Kosovo or El Salvador. Or it can be manufactured by warlords intent on enrichment, as in Bosnia. It can also, although less and less, be the result of vying interests between nation-states, such as the Gulf War, fought over control of the oil fields in Kuwait. War, at times inevitable and unavoidable, is part of human society. It has been since the dawn of time—and probably will be until we are snuffed out by our own foolishness.

"We believed we were there for a high moral purpose," wrote Philip Caputo in his book on Vietnam, *Rumor of War*. "But somehow our idealism was lost, our morals corrupted, and the purpose forgotten."[5]

The employment of organized violence means one must, in fact, abandon fixed and established values. This is a truth made apparent in *Troilus and Cressida*. It is a truth *Henry V* ignores. Once war, and especially the total war that marked both the ancient and the modern way of battle, erupts, all is sacrificed before it. The myth of war is essential to justify the horrible sacrifices required in war, the destruction and the death of innocents. It can be formed only by denying the reality of war, by turning the lies, the manipulation, the inhumanness of war into the heroic ideal. Homer did this for the Greeks, Virgil for the Augustan age, and Shakespeare for the English in his history plays. But these great writers also understood what they were doing, and thus in the canon of their works come moments when war is laid bare.

Troilus, at the start of the play, states that he will not fight for Helen, a woman portrayed by Shakespeare as a mindless paramour. "It is," he says, "too starved a subject for my sword."[6] Dying for this Helen, who has neither morals nor wit, is absurd. Yet I have seen men fight for even more ridiculous reasons. There was no reason for the war in Bosnia. The warring sides invented national myths and histories designed to mask the fact that Croats, Muslims, and Serbs are nearly indistinguishable. It was absurd nuances that propelled the war, invented historical wrongs, which, as in the Middle East, stretched back to dubious accounts of ancient history. I have heard Israeli settlers on the

West Bank, for example, argue that Palestinian towns, towns that have been Muslim since the seventh century, belong to them because it says so in the Bible, a reminder that this sophistry extends beyond the Balkans.

The competing nationalist propaganda in Yugoslavia created a conflict in the country best equipped of all the Eastern European states to integrate with the West after the collapse of communism. Because there was no real reason to fight, there was an urgent need to swiftly turn a senseless fratricide, one organized by criminals and third-rate political leaders for power and wealth, into an orgy of killing, torture, and mass execution. This indiscriminate murder, these campaigns of ethnic cleansing, were used to create facts, as it were. The slaughter was carried out to give to these wars the justifications they lacked when they began, to fuel mutual hatred and paranoia, as well as to enrich the militias and paramilitary groups that stole and looted from their victims. Ethnic warfare is a business, and the Mercedes and mansions of the warlords in Belgrade prove it. Fighting for a Helen who is a strumpet, or Don Quixote's Dulcinea, looks noble by comparison.

The cast of warlords in the former Yugoslavia was made up of the dregs of Yugoslav society. These thieves, embezzlers, petty thugs, and even professional killers swiftly became war heroes. They were, at least, colorful, with Captain Dragan, a Serbian soldier of fortune who was allegedly an ex-convict from Australia; the fascist demagogue Vojislav Šešelj; and Zeljko Ražnjatović, known as Arkan, who had a criminal record in several Western European countries. The Croats had their own collection of gangsters, including Branimir Glavaš, who stormed into Serbian villages with his militias and executed the Serbian civilians and the Croatian policemen who had tried to keep the nationalist mobs from killing them. The gangsters who took over Sarajevo at the start of the war to battle the Serbs were no different. Loot and power were always their primary objectives.

The conclusion of *Troilus and Cressida*—like *Macbeth* and *King Lear*—produces no catharsis. There is nothing redeeming about the Trojan War, in both Euripides and Shakespeare, just as there is nothing redeeming about any war, including the supposed good wars that we might all agree had to be fought. The Allied incendiary bombs that spread fires through Dresden and Tokyo left some 150,000 people dead. Talk not of the good war to those in Hiroshima or Nagasaki. It does not mean the bombing of Dresden or the dropping of the atomic bombs was wrong, given the concept of total war—a concept that would not be alien to the victorious Greeks in Troy. It means that we are naïve to ignore these and countless other events, to ennoble indiscriminate slaughter and industrial killing on so vast a scale. Modern war is directed primarily against civilians. Look at Kosovo, Bosnia, Rwanda, Vietnam, or World War II. And nuclear terrorism is the logical outcome of modern industrial warfare.

"Let it be said then that I wrote this book in the absolute conviction that there never has been, nor ever can be, a 'good' or worthwhile war," wrote the Canadian World War II veteran Farley Mowat. "Mine was one of the better ones (as such calamities are measured), but still, a bloody awful thing it was. So awful that through three decades I kept the deeper agonies of it wrapped in the cotton-wool of protective forgetfulness, and would have been well content to leave them buried forever ... but could not, because the Old Lie—temporarily discredited by the Vietnam debacle—is once more gaining credence; a whisper which soon may become another strident shout urging us on to mayhem."[7]

In Homer it is the malice of the gods that propels both sides to destruction. In Shakespeare, it is the capriciousness of men. There is, at the end of *Troilus and Cressida*, one of the great scenes of war set down in literature. It is the moment when Achilles, roused to fury over the death of his companion Patroclus on the battlefield, finds Hector, unarmed, stripping the armor off the body of a Greek soldier whom he had struck down as he was fleeing the battlefield.

Shakespeare turns the scene into butchery, with the helpless Hector begging Achilles not to strike him while he has no weapon. Achilles has no chivalry. Rather than a fight between equals, it is murder, with Hector being surrounded and struck by a swarm of Achilles' Myrmidon soldiers.

ACHILLES:

> Look, Hector, how the sun begins to set,
> How ugly night comes breathing at his heels;
> Even with the vail and dark'ning of the sun,
> To close the day up. Hector's life is done.

HECTOR:

> I am unarm'd, forgo this vantage.

ACHILLES:

> Strike, fellows, strike, this is the man I seek.
> So, Ilion, fall thou next! Come, Troy, sink down!
> Here lies thy heart, thy sinews, and thy bone.
> On Myrmidons, and cry you all amain,
> "Achilles hath the mighty Hector slain!"[8]

Moments after Hector's death dozens of heavily armed men thrust spears into Hector's corpse. Achilles commands his Myrmidons to cry out to the Greeks that he "hath the mighty Hector slain." Here is the lie of the heroic ideal, an ideal we nurture, despite centuries of war. Here is the instant creation of heroic myth, out of murder. Here also we see the mutilation of the dead that has been part of military behavior since there were men in arms. If you kill your enemy his body becomes your trophy, your possession, and this has been a fundamental part of warfare since before the Philistines beheaded Saul.

In Bosnia there was a local Croat warlord who rode around his village with the skull of the local imam for a hood ornament. In El Salvador government soldiers sometimes carried photos of themselves squatted around the body of a rebel killed in a firefight.

History for Shakespeare was not the example of the inner workings of the divine or the fodder for some generalized principle. It was merely itself. It moved toward no goal. Shakespeare understood the monstrous, deadly neutrality of nature.

"Those who believe that God himself, once he became man, could not face the harshness of destiny without a long tremor of anguish," Simone Weil writes, "should have understood that the only people who can give the impression of having risen to a higher plane, who seem superior to ordinary human misery, are the people who resort to the aids of illusion, exaltation, fanaticism, to conceal the harshness of destiny from their own eyes. The man who does not wear the armor of the lie cannot experience force without being touched by it to the very soul."⁹

And when the rhetoric of war is long forgot, what happens to the heroic dead, the bereaved mothers, fathers, husbands, wives, and children of those killed and lost? What comes of those who made, in the glib term of politicians, the supreme sacrifice?

A passage from the November 18, 1822, *London Observer* caught the aftermath of war:

It is estimated that more than a million bushels of human and inhuman bones were imported last year from the continent of Europe into the port of Hull. The neighborhood of Leipzig, Austerlitz, Waterloo, and of all the places where, during the late bloody war, the principal battles were fought, have been swept alike of the bones of the hero and the horse which he rode. Thus collected from every quarter, they have been shipped to the port of Hull and thence forwarded to the Yorkshire bone grinders who have erected steam-engines and powerful machinery for the purpose of reducing them to a granularly state. In this condition they are sold to the farmers to manure their lands.[10]

In World War I, on the Western Front, the petrifying and decomposed dead lay draped on the barbed wire and rotting in gaping shell holes. Half a million British dead in World War I were never found, and this number was dwarfed by the missing Russians, Germans, Austrians, and French. The earth consumed them, just as at Waterloo, as in all battles. They vanished as swiftly as the eternal causes for which they were sacrificed. They were replaced by a new generation and new causes. In the light of time, what looked so momentous then now looks like folly.

In *Life in the Tomb*, the Greek author Stratis Myrivilis, who fought in the Balkans in World War I, writes,

A few years from now, I told him, perhaps others would be killing each other for anti-nationalist ideals. Then they would laugh at our own killings just as we had laughed at those of the Byzantines. These others would indulge in mutual slaughter with the same enthusiasm, though their ideals were new. Warfare under the entirely fresh banners would be just as disgraceful as always. They might even rip out each other's guts then with religious zeal, claiming that they were "fighting to end all fighting." But they too would be followed by still others who would laugh at them with the same gusto.[11]

Nationalist and ethnic conflicts are fratricides that turn on absurdities. They can only be sustained by myth. The arguments and bloody disputes take place over tiny, almost imperceptible nuances within the society—what Sigmund Freud calls the "narcissism of minor differences."[12] In the Balkans, for example, there were heated debates over the origin of gingerbread hearts—cookies in the shape of hearts. The Croats insisted that the cookies were Croatian. The Serbs angrily countered that the cookies were Serbian. The suggestion to one ethnic group that gingerbread hearts were invented by the other ethnic group could start a fight. To those of us on the outside it had a Gilbert and Sullivan lunacy to it, but to the participants it was deadly serious. It had to be. For the nationalist myths stand on such minuscule differences. These myths give neighbors the justification to kill those they had gone to school and grown up with.

The Serbs, Muslims, and Croats struggled, like ants on a small hill, to carve out separate, antagonistic identities. But it was all negative space. One defined oneself mostly by what the other was not.

The term Serbo-Croatian, for example, caused great umbrage to anyone who was not a Serb. Suddenly, instead of one language called Serbo-Croatian, there were three languages in Bosnia—Bosnian, Serbian, and Croatian. And the United Nations, pandering to nationalist cant, printed public reports in all three, although the reports were nearly identical.

Spoken Serbian, Bosnian, and Croatian are of Slavic origin and have minor differences in syntax, pronunciation, and slang. The Croats and Bosnian Muslims use the Roman alphabet. The Serbs use the Cyrillic alphabet. Otherwise the tongue they all speak is nearly the same.

Since there was, in essence, one language, the Serbs, Muslims and Croats each began to distort their own tongue to accommodate the myth of separateness. The Bosnian Muslims introduced Arabic words and Koranic expressions into the language. The Muslims during the war adopted words like *shahid*, or martyr, from Arabic, dropping the Serbian word *junak*. They begun using Arabic expressions, like *inshallah* (God willing), *marhaba* (hello) and *salam alekhum* (peace be upon you).

Just as energetically the Croats swung the other way, dusting off words from the fifteenth century. The Croatian president at the time, Franjo Tudjman, took delight in inventing new terms. Croatian parliamentarians proposed passing a law that would levy fines and prison terms for those who use "words of foreign origin."

In Zagreb, the capital of Croatia, waiters and shop clerks would turn up their noses at patrons who used old "Serbian" phrases. The Education Ministry in Croatia told teachers to mark "non-Croatian" words on student papers as incorrect. The stampede to establish a "pure" Croatian language, led by a host of amateurs and politicians, resulted in chaos and rather bizarre linguistic twists.

There are two words in Serbo-Croatian, for example, for "one thousand." One of the words, *tisuca*, was not used by the Communist government that ruled the old Yugoslavia, which preferred *hiljada*, paradoxically, an archaic Croatian word. *Hiljada*, although more authentically Croatian, was discarded by

Croatian nationalists; *tisuca*, perhaps because it was banned by the Communists, was in fashion.

The movement, done in the name of authenticity, was patently artificial. It was a linguistic version of gingerbread hearts. It was a way in which a nation could find tiny specks over which to argue and establish an identity and go to war.

The campaign soon included efforts to eradicate words borrowed from English, German, and French. President Tudjman dreamed up new tennis terms to replace English ones. International judges, forced to use the president's strange sports vocabulary at tennis tournaments, stumbled over the unfamiliar words, like the unwieldy word *pripetavanje*, difficult even for Croatians, which had to be used instead of "tiebreaker."

It reached a point of such confusion that Tudjman began to slip up. When he greeted President Clinton in Zagreb he used the Serbian version of the word happy, *srecan*, rather than *sretan*, deemed to be Croatian. The gaffe, broadcast live, was quickly edited out of later news reports on the state-controlled television.

Off-duty Croatian policemen in a nightclub beat up members of a Sarajevo rock band, No Smoking, after they sang a tune with Serbian lyrics. The police, who punched and kicked the musicians, had taken offense at the Serbian word *delija,* which means "a cool dude."

It was not the first time that the Croatian authorities tried to create a politically appropriate lexicon. In 1941, the fascist war leader in Zagreb, Ante Pavelić, also banned all words he deemed not to be of Croatian origin. Nor was this unique to the former Yugoslavia. The hijacking of language is fundamental to war. It becomes difficult to express contrary opinions. There are simply not the words or phrases to do it. We all speak with the same clichés and euphemisms.

The myth of war creates a new, artificial reality. Moral precepts—ones we have spent a lifetime honoring—are jettisoned. We accept, if not condone, the maiming and killing of others as the regrettable cost of war. We operate under a new moral code.

The political left in America and Europe, the intellectuals and artists, those who spent a lifetime outside of the mainstream, are equally susceptible. Many were rarely content with simply denouncing American foreign policy in places like Central America or the Middle East—a stance for which I have some sympathy—but had to embrace opposition forces with stunning credulity.

During the Spanish Civil War George Orwell observed that "The thing that was truly frightening about the war in Spain was ... the immediate reappearance in left-wing circles of the mental atmosphere of the Great War. The very people who for 20 years sniggered over their own superiority to war hysteria were the ones who rushed straight back into the mental slum of 1915."[13]

By supporting "revolutionary" movements in El Salvador or Nicaragua these social critics found a balm for their alienation. They were able to revel in the intoxication of force and still express an antagonism towards American policy. These groups, like fellow travelers before them in the Soviet Union or Cuba, swallowed whole the utopian vision of opposition or revolutionary movements, ignoring the messier realities of internal repression and war crimes. It was not unusual to find political pilgrims who had toured Nicaragua or Gaza overwhelmed with emotion. They poured superlatives on the oppressed people they championed, although once the conflicts ended the lionized peoples of Bosnia, Nicaragua, or El Salvador were usually forgotten.

During the height of the war in Nicaragua these groups

descended frequently on the country. They were nicknamed "the sandalistas" by critics because of their penchant for dressing in ratty attire and sandals. I spent a day with one group that, the first day they arrived, headed straight to the U.S. Embassy for a protest rally.

"For me," said one of the participants, "a demonstration at the embassy will be my liturgy for the morning."

"Amen," said one of her fifteen companions.

The group was part of a religious organization from Dayton, Ohio, known as Pledge of Resistance. They would return to Ohio to speak in church basements and at small gatherings about their experiences in Nicaragua. The trip, organized by a group known as Witness for Peace, took the members to a model prison farm, arranged interviews with Sandinista supporters, and threw in several moderate critics.

Alvaro José Baldizón, the former chief investigator of the Special Investigations Commission of the Ministry of Interior, told me after he had fled to the United States that before one of the solidarity groups arrived in a town, critics were warned by police to stay away from the foreigners. He said that government employees often posed as local residents or relatives of local residents and spoke about atrocities carried out by the Contras as well as the benefits of the Sandinista revolution. The two-week visits saw most groups live for a few days in a village. They held prayer vigils, did work projects, and collected testimony from alleged victims of the war.

I went with the group to a model prison farm. It had pleasant gardens and spotless sleeping quarters. The farm housed forty-two inmates. The group was told that there were only two unarmed guards on the farm, prisoners were given a one-week vacation, and no one had ever tried to escape.

A prisoner, Hernán Lozano, who said he was once a body-guard for the former dictator Anastasio Somoza, spoke to the delegation. I would hear a version of this talk from dozens of other prisoners. The stocky Lozano grinned lavishly and heaped praise on the Sandinistas.

"You appear happy to be here," said one of the Americans. "Are you truly happy or is this an appearance?"

Lozano assured the delegation he was happy on the prison farm. He told them he was telling the truth because "the revolution has brought the loss of fear, especially the fear of telling the truth."

The Potemkin quality of the farm seemed hard to miss even for the delegates.

"Even if this is a showpiece, the cream of the crop, it is here," another participant told me. "It does seem to be more than good intentions. In reality it is a lot better than in our own country."

The group, often praised by Sandinista officials for their courage and dedication, became openly moved at the end of the day. There was an electric current of self-satisfaction and moral outrage that ran concurrently through the conversation.

"To me, the process of the revolution is a religious experience. It's not a political movement," said another American in the group. "It comes from a deep-faith commitment by the Nicaraguan people."

The social critic Christopher Lasch has argued that such radical politics fills empty lives and provides a potent sense of meaning and purpose. It is "a refuge from the terrors of inner life," he observed in *The Culture of Narcissism*.[14]

But it is a refuge for all, for lower classes as well as privileged elite. None of us is immune. All find emotional sustenance in war's myth. That myth can take many forms. It can lead people to celebrate power among those who are America's enemies, those who lead "revolutionary" regimes in Cuba or Vietnam, or it can lead us to celebrate our own power, but the process is the same. It is still myth. It still blinds those who swallow it.

The myth of war rarely endures for those who experience combat. War is messy, confusing, sullied by raw brutality and an elephantine fear that grabs us like a massive bouncer who comes up from behind. Soldiers in the moments before real battles weep, vomit, and write last letters home, although these are done more as a precaution than from belief. All are nearly paralyzed with fright. There is a morbid silence that grips a battlefield in the final moments before the shooting starts, one that sets the back of my own head pounding in pain, wipes away all appetite, and makes my fingers tremble as I ready myself to go forward against logic. You do not think of home or family, for to do so is to be overcome by a wave of nostalgia and emotion that can impair your ability to survive. One thinks, so far as it is possible, of cleaning weapons, of readying for the business of killing. No one ever charges into battle for God and country.

"Just remember," a Marine Corps lieutenant colonel told me as he strapped his pistol belt under his arm before we crossed into Kuwait, "that none of these boys is fighting for home, for the flag, for all that crap the politicians feed the public. They are fighting for each other, just for each other."

It may be that Falstaff, rather than Henry V, is a much more accurate picture of the common soldier, who finds little in the rhetoric of officers who urge him into danger. The average soldier probably sympathizes more than we might suspect with Falstaff's stratagems to save his own hide. Falstaff embodies the carnal yearnings we all have for food, drink, companionship, a few sexual adventures, and safety. He may lack the essential comradeship of soldiering, but he clings to life in a way a soldier under fire can sympathize with. It is to the pubs and taverns, not to the grand palaces, that these soldiers return when the war is done. And Falstaff's selfish lust for pleasure hurts few. Henry's selfish lust for power leaves corpses strewn across muddy battlefields.[15]

The imagined heroism, the vision of a dash to rescue a wounded comrade, the clear lines we thought were drawn in battle, the images we have of our own reaction under gunfire, usually wilt in combat. This is a sober and unsettling realization. We may not be who we thought we would be. One of the most difficult realizations of war is how deeply we betray ourselves, how far we are from the image of gallantry and courage we desire, how instinctual and primordial fear is. We do not meditate on action. Our movements are usually motivated by a numbing and overpowering desire for safety. And yet there are heroes, those who somehow rise above it all, maybe only once, to expose themselves to risk to save their comrades. I have seen such soldiers. I nearly always found them afterward to be embarrassed about what they did, unable to explain it, reticent to talk. Many are not sure they could do it again.

I was in Khartoum in 1989 during one of the attempts to overthrow Sadek Mahdi, who was then the prime minister. The city had fallen into decay, with lines of destitute Sudanese curled up in blankets and with holes in the pitted roads so huge that men fell into them. Electricity and water service were sporadic. The phones did not work. The only thing that seemed to function was the rampant corruption. The coup attempt had been fought off, but the army was still nervous. At dusk another reporter and I took a walk through the streets. Inadvertently, we turned down the road past the Presidential Palace. In the half-light the palace guards, who had ordered the road closed to all traffic and pedestrians, noisily unlocked the safeties on their assault rifles and pointed their weapons toward us. We yelled out in Arabic, "Foreigners! Foreigners!" I deftly, without hesitation or forethought, sidestepped behind my friend. Better to let any bullets pass through him first. It was a disconcerting decision, one made swiftly and instinctually. To this day I have not had the heart to tell him.

We are humiliated when under fire. In combat the abstract words of glory, honor, courage often become obscene and empty. They are replaced by the tangible images of war, the names of villages, mountains, roads, dates, and battalions that mean nothing to the outsider but pack enormous emotional power and fear to those caught up in the combat.

Once in a conflict, we are moved from the abstract to the real, from the mythic to the sensory. When this move takes place we have nothing to do with a world not at war. When we return home we view the society around us from the end of a very long tunnel. There they still believe. In combat such belief is shattered, replaced not with a better understanding, but with a disconcerting confusion and a taste of war's potent and addictive narcotic. Combatants live only for their herd, those hapless soldiers who are bound into their unit to ward off death. There is no world outside the unit. It alone endows worth and meaning. Soldiers will rather die than betray this bond. And there is—as many combat veterans will tell you—a kind of love in this.

The Salvadoran town of Suchitoto was a dreary peasant outpost made up of stucco and mud and wattle huts. It was off the main road. The town was surrounded by the Farabundo Marti National Liberation Front (FMLN) rebels, who, when I first arrived in El Salvador in 1982, were winning the war. The government forces kept a small garrison in the town, although its relief columns were regularly ambushed as they ambled down the small strip of asphalt, surrounded by high grass. It was one of the most dangerous spots in El Salvador and had taken the lives of a few reporters.

The rebels launched an attack to take the town. A convoy of reporters in cars marked with "TV" in masking tape on the windshields hightailed it to the small bridge that led to the lonely stretch of road into Suchitoto. We stopped for the familiar ritual of getting high, something as a print reporter who could scramble to safety I did not do, but something many photographers, who would stand and take pictures in the midst of combat, found a necessary salve to their nerves.

Then we moved slowly down the road, the odd round fired ahead or behind us. We made it to the edge of town. We ran into rebel units, now accustomed to the follies of the press. On foot we moved through the deserted streets, the firing from the garrison becoming louder as we weaved our way with rebel fighters to the front line. And then, as we rounded a corner, several full bursts of automatic fire rent the air. We dove head-first onto the dirt. The rebels began to fire noisy bursts from their M–16 assault rifles. The acrid scent of cordite filled the air. Dust was in my eyes. I did not move. I began to pray.

"God," I though, "if you get me out of here I will never do this again."

I felt powerless, humiliated, weak. I dared not move. I could see the little sprays of dust the bullets threw up from the road. Rebels around me were wounded and crying out in pain. One died yelling out in a sad cadence for his mother. His desperate and final plea seemed to cut through the absurd posturing of soldiering. At first it haunted me. Soon I wished he would be quiet.

"Mama!" . . . "Mama!" . . . "Mama!"

The firefight seemed to go on for an eternity. I cannot say how long I lay there. It could have been a few minutes. It could have been an hour. Here was war, real war, sensory war, not the war of the movies and books I had consumed in my youth. It was disconcerting, frightening, and disorganized, and nothing like the myth I had been peddled. There was nothing gallant or heroic, nothing redeeming. It controlled me. I would never control it.

During a lull I dashed across an empty square and found shelter behind a house. My heart was racing. Adrenaline coursed through my bloodstream. I was safe. I made it back to the capital. And, like most war correspondents, I soon considered the experience a great cosmic joke. I drank away the fear and excitement in a seedy bar in downtown San Salvador. Most people after such an experience would learn to stay away. I was hooked.

2

THE PLAGUE
OF NATIONALISM

War is the health of the state.

·

RANDOLPH BOURNE

THE MILITARY JUNTA THAT RULED ARGENTINA, AND WAS
responsible for killing 20,000 of its own citizens during the
"Dirty War," in 1982 invaded the Falkland Islands, which the
Argentines called the Malvinas. The junta, which had been on
the verge of collapse and beset by violent street demonstrations
and nationwide strikes in the weeks before the war, instantly
became the saviors of the country. Labor union and opposition
leaders, some of whom were still visibly bruised from beatings,
were hauled out of jail cells before cameras to repeat what was
a collective mantra: "Las Malvinas son Argentinas."

The invasion transformed the country. Reality was replaced
with a wild and self-serving fiction, a legitimization of the worst
prejudices of the masses and paranoia of the outside world.
The secret interior world arrayed against Argentina became one

of strange cabals, worldwide Jewry trotted out again to be beaten like an old horse, vast subterranean webs that had as their focus the destruction of the Argentine people. The exterior world was exemplified by the nation. All that was noble and good was embodied, like some unique gene, in the Argentine people. Stories of the heroism of the Argentine military—whose singular recent accomplishment was the savage repression of its own people—filled the airwaves.

Friends of mine, who a few days earlier had excoriated the dictatorship, now bragged about the prowess of Argentine commanders. One general, during a dispute with Chile, flew his helicopter over the Chilean border in order to piss on Chilean soil. This story was repeated with evident pride. Cars raced through the city streets honking horns and waving the blue and white Argentine flag. Argentines burst into the national anthem and ecstatic cheering at sporting events. The large Anglo-Argentine community sent delegations to Britain to lobby for the junta.

I had spent nights with Argentine friends talking of a new Argentina, one that would respect human rights, allow basic freedoms, and perhaps put on trial the generals responsible for the Dirty War. Now such talk was an anathema, even treasonous. On the street any dissent, especially from a foreigner, could mean physical violence. Any suggestion that the invasion was not just and correct and glorious was unpalatable. One never referred to the islands by their English name. Overweening pride and a sense of national solidarity swept through the city like an electric current. It was as if I had woken up, like one of Kafka's characters, and found myself transformed into a huge bug. I would come to feel this way in every nation at war, including in the United States after the attacks of September 11.

This was my first taste of nationalist triumphalism in wartime. There was almost no one I could speak with. A populace that had agitated for change now outdid itself to lionize uniformed killers. All bowed before the state. It taught me a crucial lesson that I would carry into every other conflict. Lurking beneath the surface of every society, including ours, is the passionate yearning for a nationalist cause that exalts us, the kind that war alone is able to deliver. It reduces and at times erases the anxiety of individual consciousness. We abandon individual responsibility for a shared, unquestioned communal enterprise, however morally dubious.

There is little that logic or fact or truth can do to alter the experience. Moreover, once this crusade is embraced by the nation, the myth predetermines how the world is perceived. It is only after the myth implodes, often as suddenly as it descended, that one can again question the motives and the actions of the state. Once the lights are flicked on again there is a *Midsummer Night's Dream* quality to the war experience, as if no one can quite remember what happened.

"The nationalist is by definition an ignoramus," wrote Danilo Kiš, the Yugoslav writer. "Nationalism is the line of least resistance, the easy way. The nationalist is untroubled, he knows or thinks he knows what his values are, his, that's to say national, that's to say the values of the nations he belongs to, ethical and political; he is not interested in others, *they are of no concern of his,* hell—it's other people (other nations, another tribe). They don't even need investigating. The nationalist sees other people in his own image—as nationalists."[1]

Every society, ethnic group or religion nurtures certain myths, often centered around the creation of the nation or the movement itself. These myths lie unseen beneath the surface, waiting for the moment to rise ascendant, to define and glorify followers or members in times of crisis. National myths are largely benign in times of peace. They are stoked by the entertainment industry, in school lessons, stories, and quasi-historical ballads, preached in mosques, or championed in absurd historical dramas that are always wildly popular during war. They do not pose a major challenge to real historical study or a studied tolerance of others in peacetime. But national myths ignite a collective amnesia in war. They give past generations a nobility and greatness they never possessed. Almost every group, and especially every nation, has such myths. These myths are the kindling nationalists use to light a conflict.

In the former Yugoslavia, it was the nationalist propaganda pumped out over television, far more than ancient hatreds, that did the most to provoke rivalry and finally war between ethnic groups. The nationalist governments, rather than allow for the discussion of competing ideas and viewpoints, used the absolute power they wielded over the broadcast media to play and replay images that provoked outrage and anger. They told stories, many of them fabricated, about alleged atrocities committed by the enemy. Impartial information disappeared. Television became the emotional crutch used to justify violence and rally ethnic groups around nationalist leaders. Those who advocated violence were affirmed, night after night, in their righteous anger. The principal religious institutions—the Serbian Orthodox Church and the Catholic Church in Croatia—were willing accomplices. They were national churches and worked as propagandists for the state. The clerics, on all three sides, were a disgrace. U.N. mediators in Sarajevo wearily complained that it was easier to get Serb and Muslim commanders to the table for talks than opposing clerics.

Archeology, folklore, and the search for what is defined as

authenticity are the tools used by nationalists to assail others and promote themselves. They dress it up as history, but it is myth. Real historical inquiry, in the process, is corrupted, assaulted, and often destroyed. Facts become as interchangeable as opinions. Those facts that are inconvenient are discarded or denied. The obvious inconsistencies are ignored by those intoxicated by a newly found sense of national pride and the exciting prospect of war.

To speak of the Israeli war of independence with many Israelis, in which stateless European Jews established a country in a land that had been primarily Muslim since the seventh century, is to shout into a vast black hole. There is an emotional barrier, a desire not to tarnish the creation myth, which makes it difficult for many Israeli Jews, including some of the most liberal and progressive, to acknowledge the profound injustice the creation of the state of Israel meant for Palestinians. As Americans we struggle with these myths as well, only grudgingly conceding that many of our founding fathers were slave owners and much of our nation acquired after a genocidal campaign against Native Americans.

In peacetime this collective amnesia is challenged by a few intrepid scholars. Indeed, some of the best scholarly work on the 1948 war and what it meant for the Palestinians has come from Israeli historians—but their voices are muted or silenced in times of crisis. Our own nation is no different. We embrace gross and overtly racist notions of Islam that paint all Muslims as having a tendency to violence, anger, antimodernism, and close-mindedness. Questioning of the nationalist line, or an attempt to address historical injustices committed by us against our foes, is branded unpatriotic, intellectual treason, just as it was in Argentina in 1982.

Intellectuals and social critics are as susceptible to the plague of nationalism as the masses. They often find in it an answer to their own feelings of ostracism. In the nationalist cause they are given a chance to be exalted by a nation that has ignored them. They too enjoy intoxication. There are no shortages of intellectuals willing to line up behind leaders they despise in times of national crisis, an act that negates the moral posturing they often make from within the confines of academia during peacetime. These enthusiastic intellectuals can become dangerous in wartime. Many hold messianic and uncompromising beliefs that they have never had to put into practice. All nationalist movements have such pernicious mentors willing to justify the use of force for a utopian and unworkable vision. Among the Serbs Dobrica Ćosić, whose sentimental novels about Serbian heroism during World War I found a wide following, including Milošević, was able to replace real history with Serbian nationalist myth, which was used to fuel the war.

Those who do defy the nationalist agenda in war are usually reviled during the conflict and shunned afterward. They are, at least by the labels placed upon them by the world, often rather humble, sometimes simple, and not always well educated. The acts defy the collective psychosis.

A friend of mine in Serbia, Slavica, had a former Muslim classmate who lived in Mostar, a Bosnian city that was devastated in the war by Serbian and later Croatian troops. She sent her two small children to live with Slavica, her husband, and young daughter in a town in northern Serbia. The arrival of the Muslim children caused a furor. The school did not want them to attend classes. Neighbors spat at Slavica and the children in the street. Her windows were broken. Crude graffiti was spray-painted on the walls of her home. Yet she persisted. She cared for the children as her own. After a year she got them into the school, although they endured taunts and harassment.

After the war the townspeople preferred to forget. No one apologized. Slavica was allowed to be a nominal member of the community. She told me that people were uncomfortable around her. She was a reminder of the collective cowardice and indifference by many in her town now. She, I believe, shamed those around her.

"I will never again feel a part of the country where I was born and raised," she said.

Yet Slavica also felt guilt and shame for the way her nation had reacted, although she had chosen a different response. She insisted that she and her husband had done too little, that the sheltering of the children was insignificant given the magnitude of the crimes committed in the name of the Serbs. The Muslim children, whom she eventually sent to their mother when the mother managed to get political asylum in Canada, called infrequently. They may not have wanted to remember the pain and powerlessness of such dislocation. Slavica was profoundly alone.

Many of those who defy the collective psychosis of the nation are solitary figures once the wars end. Yet these acts of compassion were usually the best antidotes to the myths peddled by nationalists. Those who reached across lines to assist the "enemy" freed themselves from nationalist abstractions that dehumanized others. They were vaccinated against the cult of death that dominates societies in wartime. They reduced their moral universe to caring for another human being. And in this they were able to reject the messianic pretensions that come with the nationalist agenda. By accepting that they could only affect a few lives they also accepted their small place in the universe. This daily lesson in humility protected them. They were saved not by what they could accomplish but by faith. Such people are, however, very rare.

"The survivors all suffer from the same certainty: they know that if similar acts of persecution were to begin tomorrow, despite all the official demonstrations of sympathy for the victims and condemnation of the oppressors, the rescuers would be as rare as they were before," wrote Tzvetan Todorov in *Facing the Extreme: Moral Life in the Concentration Camps.* "Their good neighbors who now greet them every morning would once again turn away."[2]

I sat one afternoon with a Bosnian Serb couple, Rosa and Drago Sorak, outside of the Muslim enclave of Goražde where they had once lived. They poured out the usual scorn on the Muslims, but then stopped at the end of the rant and told me that not all Muslims were bad. This, they said, it was their duty to admit.

During the fighting in the bleak, bombed-out shell of a city that was Goražde, where bands of children had become street urchins and hundreds of war-dead lay in hastily dug graves, a glimmer of humanity arrived for the Soraks in the shape of Fadil Fejzić's cow. The cow forged an unusual bond between Fejzić, a Muslim, and his Serbian neighbors, the Soraks.

When the Serbs began the siege of Goražde in 1992, the Soraks lived in the city with their older son, Zoran, and his wife. They were indifferent, although they were Serbs, to the nationalist propaganda of Bosnian Serb leaders like Radovan Karadžić.

After Serbian forces began to shell the city and cut off the electricity, gas, and water, the family refused to move out. They threw their lot in with the Bosnian government and were branded by the Bosnian Serbs, who pounded them each day from the mountains above the town, as traitors.

On the night of June 14, 1992, the Bosnian police came to

the door for Zoran, who until the war was on Yugoslavia's national handball team.

"The Muslim police said they were taking him away for interrogation," said Drago Sorak, "but he never came back. We went nearly every day to the police station, until we left Goražde, to beg for information. They told us nothing. We assume he is dead."

Soon afterward, their second son, who fought with the Bosnian Serbs, was struck by a car and killed. The Soraks were childless.

The couple, harassed by some Muslims in the town, began to consider fleeing, although it would be months before they could get out. Drago Sorak was increasingly pressed into digging trenches and chopping firewood for the Bosnian Army. The couple had little to eat.

"As things deteriorated it got worse and worse," he said. "Some of the Muslims wanted to kill us and others defended us. There were only 200 Serbs left in the city. On some nights, groups of Muslims came to the apartment looking for us. We had to hide until they left. We were frightened."

The difficulties, the harassment, and the disappearance of Zoran all helped turn the couple against a Muslim-led government that they had been willing to accept at the start of the war.

"I would live in Albania before I would go back to living with the Muslims here," Rosa Sorak said. "How can you expect us to live with those who murdered my son?"

Five months after Zoran's disappearance, his wife gave birth to a girl. The mother was unable to nurse the child. The city was being shelled continuously. There were severe food shortages. Infants, like the infirm and the elderly, were dying in droves. The family gave the baby tea for five days, but she began to fade.

"She was dying," Rosa Sorak said. "It was breaking our hearts."

Fejzić, meanwhile, was keeping his cow in a field on the eastern edge of Goražde, milking it at night to avoid being hit by Serbian snipers.

"On the fifth day, just before dawn, we heard someone at the door," said Rosa Sorak. "It was Fadil Fejzić in his black rubber boots. He handed up half a liter of milk. He came the next morning, and the morning after that, and after that. Other families on the street began to insult him. They told him to give his milk to Muslims, to let the Chetnik children die. He never said a word. He refused our money. He came for 442 days, until my daughter-in-law and granddaughter left Goražde for Serbia."

The Soraks eventually left and took over a house that once belonged to a Muslim family in the Serbian-held town of Kopaci, two miles to the east. They could no longer communicate with Fejzić.

The couple said they grieved daily for their sons. They missed their home. They said they could never forgive those who took Zoran from them. But they also said that despite their anger and loss, they could not listen to other Serbs talking about Muslims, or even recite their own sufferings, without telling of Fejzić and his cow. Here was the power of love. What this illiterate farmer did would color the life of another human being, who might never meet him, long after he was gone. In his act lay an ocean of hope.

"It is our duty to always tell this story," Drago Sorak said. "Salt, in those days, cost $80 a kilo. The milk he had was precious, all the more so because it was hard to keep animals. He gave us 221 liters. And every year at this time, when it is cold and dark, when we close our eyes, we can hear the boom of the heavy guns and the sound of Fadil Fejzić's footsteps on the stairs."

Fejzić fell on hard times after the war. I found him selling small piles of worm-eaten apples picked from abandoned orchards outside the shattered remains of an apartment block. His apartment block had been destroyed by artillery shells, leaving him to share the floor of an unheated room with several other men. His great brown-and-white milk cow, the one the Soraks told me about, did not survive the war. It was slaughtered for the meat more than a year before as the Serbian forces tightened the siege. He had only a thin, worn coat to protect him from the winter cold. When we spoke he sat huddled in the corner of a dank, concrete-walled room rubbing his pathetic collection of small apples, many with brown holes in them, against his sleeve.

When I told him I had seen the Soraks, his eyes brightened.

"And the baby?" he asked. "How is she?"

The small acts of decency by people such as Slavica, a Serb, or Fejzić, a Muslim, in wartime ripple outwards like concentric circles. These acts, unrecognized at the time, make it impossible to condemn, legally or morally, an entire people. They serve as reminders that we all have a will of our own, a will that is independent of the state or the nationalist cause. Most important, once the war is over, these people make it hard to brand an entire nation or an entire people as guilty.

"I do not understand," wrote Primo Levi. "I cannot tolerate the fact that a man should be judged not for what he is but because of the group to which he happens to belong."[3]

But these acts also remind us that in wartime most people are unwilling to risk discomfort, censure, or violence to help neighbors. There is a frightening indifference and willful blindness, a desire to believe the nationalist myth because it brands those outside a nation or ethnic group with traits and vices that cannot be eradicated. Because they are the other, because they are not us, they are guilty. Such indifference, such acceptance of nationalist self-glorification, turns many into silent accomplices.

To those who swallow the nationalist myth, life is transformed. The collective glorification permits people to abandon their usual preoccupation with the petty concerns of daily life. They can abandon even self-preservation in the desire to see themselves as players in a momentous historical drama. This vision is accepted even at the expense of self-annihilation. Life in wartime becomes theater. All are actors. Leaders, against the backdrop of war, look heroic, noble. Pilots who bail out of planes shot down by the enemy and who make their way back home play cameo roles. The state, as we saw in the Persian Gulf War or Afghanistan, transforms war into a nightly television show. The generals, who are no more interested in candor than they were in Vietnam, have at least perfected the appearance of candor. And the press has usually been more than willing to play the dupe as long as the ratings are good.

The daily wartime episodes are central to the nationalist vision. The carefully choreographed performances come to define and make up the body politic. The lines between real entertainment and political entertainment blur and finally vanish. The world, as we see it in wartime, becomes high drama. It is romanticized. A moral purpose is infused into the trivial and the commonplace. And we, who yesterday felt maligned, alienated, and ignored, are part of a nation of self-appointed agents of the divine will. We await our chance to walk on stage.

During the first protest movement against Milošević in the winter of 1998, a time when nationalism should have been discredited, I visited one of the faculties occupied by the students who sought Milošević's removal. I arrived at the front door of the Philosophy Department at Belgrade University to be stopped by several curt young men with tags on their jackets identifying them as "security."

Students inside who attempted to speak to me were told by the security detail that only "the committee" had the right to make statements. And when Jack Lang, former minister of culture in France, arrived at the building to express his support for the student protesters, he was escorted by young men in green fatigue jackets to a room where he was declared "an enemy of the Serbs" and ordered to leave.

Lang had stumbled unwittingly on the virulent Serbian nationalism that colored the anti-government protests. The incident highlighted the problem that changing Serbian society did not lie in overturning the rule of one man, but in transforming a country that had come to see racist remarks as acceptable and had learned to express itself in the language of hate and nationalist crusades. The opposition to Milošević came from those who felt he had sold out the Serbs in Croatia and Bosnia. There was no repentance.

"Students, professors, and many Serbs have simply switched their ideological iconography," Obrad Savic, the head of the Belgrade Circle, a dissident group, told me. "They have shifted from a Marxist paradigm to Serbian nationalism. We have failed to build an intellectual tradition where people think for themselves. We operate only in the collective. We speak in the plural as the Serbian people. It's frightening, especially in the young. It will take years for us to rid ourselves of this virus."

As fervently as Western reporters sought, as they often do, to recreate the students in their own image as democratic reformers, the student organizers mocked them. This was no democratic movement, just as the Muslim-dominated government in Sarajevo had no interest in recreating a multi-ethnic city. Serbian flags proliferated in the crowd and many sang "God Give Us Justice," the anthem of the old Kingdom of Yugoslavia. The students requested an audience with Patriarch Pavle, the head of the Serbian Orthodox Church, the institution that had helped give birth to the modern Serbian nationalist movement. They rejected a suggestion that they also see Belgrade's Catholic cardinal and the mufti, the leader of the tiny Islamic community.

The nationalist virus was the logical outcome of the destruction of the country's educational system that began in the 1950s under Tito's rule. Departments were purged of professors who refused to teach subjects like "Marx and Biology" and to adhere to party doctrine. Many of the best academics were blacklisted or left the country.

Following Tito's death in 1980, academics, freed from party dogma, reached out to Western intellectual traditions. But this was swiftly terminated with the rise of Serbian nationalism, an ideology that replaced the rigidity of dogmatic Marxism. By the mid–1980s the History Department, flush with the new orthodoxy, was exalting Byzantine culture and using it, instead of Marx, as a tool to bash Western liberal democracy. The works of Serbian nationalist writers were taught in literature classes, and Serbian philosophers, who espoused theories of racial superiority, including the idea that the Serbs were the oldest human race, dominated university classrooms.

The war only accelerated the decline in the educational system. More than 400,000 Serbs, many of them young and talented, left the country in the first few years of the war.

Academic standards fell as Milošević put party hacks in charge of schools and departments and sliced government spending for education.

I developed a close friendship in Belgrade with Miladin Zivotić, a leading dissident during the Communist era in Yugoslavia and one of the most prominent domestic critics of Serbian involvement in the Balkan wars. He was the leader of the Belgrade Circle, a small group of intellectuals and artists who condemned the Serbian role in the wars in Bosnia and Croatia. The groups, which he helped found in 1992 and which included Yugoslavia's best-known dissident, Milovan Djilas, tried to reach out to Muslims and Croats to create a common front against nationalist movements in the Balkans. It was often denounced by the authorities as being a tool of Serbia's enemies.

To register his disapproval of the siege of Sarajevo by the Bosnian Serbs, Zivotić visited the city in 1993 to express his solidarity with those besieged by Serb forces. He was an outspoken critic of Serbia's treatment of its ethnic minorities, especially the two million Albanians in the Kosovo region. And when nationalists began to threaten Muslims in the Sanjak region of Serbia early in the Bosnian war, he went to live with Muslim families.

"The first act any new president of this country must do is travel to Sarejevo and beg for forgiveness, just as Willy Brandt did when he traveled to Warsaw," Zivotić told me, referring to the West German chancellor who pursued a policy of reconciliation with the victims of German Nazism. "This is the only way we can heal ourselves."

Zivotić first came to prominence in 1968, when Yugoslav university students staged anti-Communist protests at the time of the Soviet-led invasion of Czechoslovakia. For their support of the students he and seven other philosophy professors were dismissed. He started the Free Belgrade University, which met secretly in houses and whose classes were often broken up by the police. He did not return to his University of Belgrade post until 1987, seven years after the death of Tito.

Soon after he regained his old position, he found himself ostracized again because of his condemnation of growing Serbian nationalism. He was attacked by students and professors for being a "traitor to the Serbian people." He retired in 1994.

"I could not stand to go to work," he said. "I had to listen to professors and students voice support and solidarity for these Bosnian fascists, Radovan Karadžić and Ratko Mladić, in the so-called Republika Srpska. It is worse now than it was under Communism. The intellectual corruption is more pervasive and profound."

He was a lonely and distraught figure. He spent his days in the offices of the Belgrade Circle headquarters, where he drank too much coffee and smoked too many cigarettes. His was a one-man crusade against nationalist madness. He was pointedly ignored by the Serbian media, who usually only quoted him after his comments appeared in my articles in *The New York Times*. The student protesters who mounted demonstrations against the Milošević government never invited him to speak, preferring to listen to rants by Serbian nationalists, who fomented the war in the first place. These speakers condemned Milošević for betraying the nationalist cause. The callous indifference of the university students hurt Zivotić tremendously.

He died of a heart attack in 1997, a year before I left the Balkans. His loss for Serbia was tremendous, for with him went one of the few remaining moral voices in the region.

The nationalist myth often implodes with a startling ferocity. It does so after the lies and absurdities that surround it become too hard to sustain. They collapse under their own weight. The contradictions and torturous refusal to acknowledge the obvious becomes more than a society is able to bear. The collapse is usually followed by a blanket refusal, caused by shame and discomfort, to examine or acknowledge the crimes carried out in the name of nationalist cause.

By the time British forces had landed on the Falklands and were rolling over the poorly supplied and ill-clad Argentine soldiers, the Argentine public had retreated into a mythic world that was not unfamiliar to Germans in the last days of the Third Reich. There was no hint in the national press that the Argentine forces were being defeated. It appeared that the British were losing the war. When the Argentine forces surrendered it hit the country like a tidal wave.

Curiously, it was not that Argentines believed their own propaganda. Many told me that they understood that much what they saw and heard in their own press was a lie. They could tune in the BBC broadcasts. They knew what the British were saying about the war. But they assumed, with a mixture of gullibility and cynicism, that each side was lying. They preferred to pick and choose. They regularly dismissed some of their own propaganda, but not the central message—that Argentina was triumphant.

The fall of the islands sent hundreds of thousands of enraged Argentines to the Plaza de Mayo in front of the Casa Rosada in Buenos Aires to demand weapons to fight. Foreign reporters were attacked, their cars overturned and burned. When a group of toughs cornered me in an alley, I was spared when I told them I was German, a fabrication they bought—convinced, I suspect, by my blond hair.

All of that rage should have been directed against the government, but instead it was turned on the foreign conspirators who were arrayed against the Argentine nation. Even in defeat, the Argentines could not let go of the nationalist myth. The next morning the government-controlled press began to explain what happened. What happened, it said, was that Argentina had been betrayed by the United States. "We can defeat one superpower," a front-page article read, "but we can not defeat two."

And then, in the days after the defeat, the myth suddenly vanished. My Argentine friends picked up where they had left off, as if there never had been a war, as if the collective intoxication was nothing more than a bad dream, a drunken night of debauchery best forgotten and impolitic to mention. One felt dirty to bring it up. I woke up one morning after the surrender and I was no longer a freak. Argentines were again able to grasp reality and respond to it. The junta, whose members should have been imprisoned, especially given the downward spiral that soon beset the economy, was allowed to fade away. No one really wanted to be reminded of the whole affair.

The novelist Marguerite Duras, who as a member of the French resistance during World War II took part in the torture of collaborators, wrote of such a moment. "Peace is visible already," she wrote. "It's like a great darkness falling, it's the beginning of forgetting. You can see already . . . I went out, peace seemed imminent. I hurried back home, pursued by peace. It had suddenly struck me that there might be a future, that a foreign land was going to emerge out of this chaos where no one would wait any more."[4]

This blanket amnesia is often part of the aftermath of war. The puncturing of the nationalist myth, an event that saw the Serbs turn their back on Milošević once Kosovo was lost, does not mean, however, that the nationalist virus has been conquered. While the excesses carried out in the name of the nationalist cause are forgotten or ignored, the myth of the nation has a disturbing longevity. It lies dormant, festering in the society, nurtured by boys' adventure stories of heroism in service to the nation, the monuments we erect to the fallen, and carefully scripted remembrances until it slowly slouches back into respectability.

Nationalist triumphalism was shunned and discredited in America after Vietnam. We were forced to see ourselves as others saw us, and it was not always pleasant. We understood, at least for a moment, the lie. But the plague of nationalism was resurrected during the Reagan years. It became ascendant with the Persian Gulf War, when we embraced the mythic and unachievable goal of a "New World Order." The infection of nationalism now lies unchecked and blindly accepted in the march we make as a nation towards another war, one as ill conceived as the war we lost in southeast Asia.

3

THE DESTRUCTION
OF CULTURE

The first casualty when war comes is truth.

•

SENATOR HIRAM JOHNSON

1917

IN WARTIME THE STATE SEEKS TO DESTROY ITS OWN
culture. It is only when this destruction has been completed
that the state can begin to exterminate the culture of its opponents. In times of conflict authentic culture is subversive. As the
cause championed by the state comes to define national identity,
as the myth of war entices a nation to glory and sacrifice, those
who question the value of the cause and the veracity of the
myths are branded internal enemies.

Art takes on a whole new significance in wartime. War and
the nationalist myth that fuels it are the purveyors of low culture—folklore, quasi-historical dramas, kitsch, sentimental dog-
gerel, and theater and film that portray the glory of soldiers in
past wars or current wars dying nobly for the homeland. This
is why so little of what moves us during wartime has any cur-

rency once war is over. The songs, books, poems, and films that arouse us in war are awkward and embarrassing when the conflict ends, useful only to summon up the nostalgia of war's comradeship.

States at war silence their own authentic and humane culture. When this destruction is well advanced they find the lack of critical and moral restraint useful in the campaign to exterminate the culture of their opponents. By destroying authentic culture—that which allows us to question and examine ourselves and our society—the state erodes the moral fabric. It is replaced with a warped version of reality. The enemy is dehumanized; the universe starkly divided between the forces of light and the forces of darkness. The cause is celebrated, often in overt religious forms, as a manifestation of divine or historical will. All is dedicated to promoting and glorifying the myth, the nation, the cause.

The works of the writers in Serbia, such as Danilo Kiš and Milovan Djilas, were mostly unavailable during the war. It remains hard even now to find their books. In Croatia the biting satires of Miroslav Krleža, who wrote one of the most searing portraits of Balkan despots, were forgotten. Writers and artists were inconvenient. They wrote about social undercurrents that were ignored by a new crop of self-appointed nationalist historians, political scientists, and economists.

National symbols—flags, patriotic songs, sentimental dedications—invade and take over cultural space. Art becomes infected with the platitudes of patriotism. More important, the use of a nation's cultural resources to back up the war effort is essential to mask the contradictions and lies that mount over time in the drive to sustain war. Cultural or national symbols that do not support the crusade are often ruthlessly removed.

In Bosnia the ethnic warlords worked hard to wipe out all the records of cohabitation between ethnic groups. The symbols of the old communist regime—one whose slogan was "Brotherhood and Unity"—were defaced or torn down. The monuments to partisan fighters who died fighting the Germans in World War II, the lists of names clearly showing a mix of ethnic groups, were blown up in Croatia. The works of Ivo Andrić, who wrote some of the most lyrical passages about a multiethnic Bosnia, were edited by the Bosnian Serbs and selectively quoted to support ethnic cleansing.

All groups looked at themselves as victims—the Croats, the Muslims, and the Serbs. They ignored the excesses of their own and highlighted the excesses of the other in gross distortions that fueled the war. The cultivation of victimhood is essential fodder for any conflict. It is studiously crafted by the state. All cultural life is directed to broadcast the injustices carried out against us. Cultural life soon becomes little more than the drivel of agitprop. The message that the nation is good, the cause just, and the war noble is pounded into the heads of citizens in everything from late-night talk shows to morning news programs to films and popular novels. The nation is soon thrown into a trance from which it does not awake until the conflict ends. In parts of the world where the conflict remains unresolved, this trance can last for generations.

I walked one morning a few years ago down the deserted asphalt tract that slices through the center of the world's last divided capital, Nicosia, on the island of Cyprus. At one spot on the asphalt dividing line was a small painted triangle. For fifteen minutes each hour, Turkish troops, who control the northern part of the island, were allowed to move from their border posts and stand inside the white triangular lines. The arrangement was part of a deal laboriously negotiated by the United

Nations to give Greek Cypriots and Turkish Cypriots access to several disputed areas along the 110-mile border that separates the north from the south. The triangle was a potent reminder that once the folly of war is over, folly itself is often all that remains.

"It's really a game of hopscotch," said Major Richard Nixon-Eckersall, a British peacekeeper who was escorting me. "You see, the Greek sentries, over there, can't see the lines. Are the Turks inside the lines or not? A lot of rock-throwing and insults are generated over this triangle. Last year the Greeks fired off five rounds at the Turks. This is considered one of the most volatile areas along the Green Line."

A buffer zone along the Green Line, set up after the Turkish invasion of Cyprus in 1974 and patrolled by United Nations soldiers, has prevented the resumption of a civil war that began in 1963. The zone—four miles wide in spots, narrowing to just a few yards in others—cuts through farmland, mountain passes, and Nicosia itself. Many of the houses and shops in the no-man's-land have dusty and decaying furniture and goods still stacked inside. Some doors have signs warning of booby traps. The deserted Nicosia International Airport with its gutted terminals, the seaside resort of Varosha swallowed up in thick vegetation, and the whitewashed Olympus Hotel were crumbling from neglect and inhabited by stray dogs and cats.

The buffer zone was lined with earthworks, barbed wire, trenches, bunkers, and watchtowers manned by troops with automatic weapons. There were about 43,000 Turkish and Greek Cypriot troops, including 30,000 Turkish soldiers sent by Ankara to the island, stationed along it.

On one side is Northern Cyprus, with one-fifth of the island's 650,000 people and a government recognized only by

Turkey. It is a dreary collection of towns and villages that look like working-class districts in Ankara or Istanbul. It suffers from constant shortages and high rates of unemployment. It is propped up by the Ankara government with an estimated $200 million a year.

The south, by contrast, has a per capita income of $12,000 a year, equal to those of Ireland or Spain. Luxury hotels and shops selling designer clothes, bone china, and computer software nestle along tree-lined avenues.

As if the war had ended only a few days ago, the Greek Cypriots and the Turkish Cypriots denounce each other in repetitive weekly editorials and political rallies. The Ayios Demetrios Church in Nicosia, in one of the stream of Greek exhibitions portraying Turkish perfidy, had just mounted a photo display of the desecration of more than 200 Greek churches in the northern part of the island. The island is hostage to its own hatred.

"For over twenty years our young men have been trained in the art of war," the Greek Cypriot president, Glafkos Clerides, told me as we chatted in his hilltop palace. "They are trained not to fight an external foe, but an internal enemy. This has had a devastating effect on the younger generation."

The war between the Orthodox Serbs and the Muslims in the Balkans was viewed by many on the island as an extension of the global religious clash that grips Cyprus. The mayor in northern Nicosia, whose father disappeared in the violence in 1963, had a poster denouncing the siege of Sarajevo on his office door.

United Nations officials, along with Greek Cypriot and Turkish Cypriot leaders, warned it would take little to trigger the conflict again.

"The two peoples cannot be put back together," said Rauf Denktash, the leader of the Turkish Cypriots, when I crossed the Green Line to see him. "One single incident, one crime involving a Turk and a Greek, would ignite the whole thing. We can't play with the fears of the people."

The white glare of the Mediterranean sun beat down on the Ledra Palace Hotel checkpoint. Only foreign visitors who do not have Turkish or Greek names can cross. At the checkpoint the Greek Cypriots and the Turkish Cypriots had set up competing billboards. Each side displayed gruesome photos of the atrocities they had allegedly endured. It was, once again, the struggle by opposing sides to wrap themselves in the mantle of victimhood. For once a group or a nation establishes that it alone suffers, then all other competing claims to injustice are canceled out. The nation or the group falls into a collective "autism," to use a phrase coined by Hans Magnus Enzensberger, and does not listen to those outside the inner circle. Communication is impossible.

"Enjoy yourself in this land of racial purity and true apartheid," read a billboard directed at those headed to the north. "Enjoy the sight of our desecrated churches. Enjoy what remains of our looted heritage and homes."

The red and white star-and-crescent flags flapped over the Turkish Cypriot guard posts, about 400 yards away, and a sign welcomed me to the Turkish Republic of Northern Cyprus.

An enlarged photo showed the bloody bodies of a Turkish Cypriot mother and her three children in a bathtub. Another showed a priest firing a rifle with the awkward English caption "A Greek Cypriot priest who forgot his religious duties and joined to the hunting of Turks."

Like the Cypriots, the Palestinians have been nurtured on bit-

ter accounts of abuse, despair, and injustice. Families tell and
retell stories of being thrown off their land and of relatives
killed or exiled. All can tick off the names of martyrs within
their own clan who died for the elusive Palestinian state. The
only framed paper in many Palestinians' homes is a sepia land
deed from the time of the British mandate. Some elderly men
still keep the keys to houses that have long since vanished.
From infancy, Palestinians are inculcated with myopic nationalism and the burden of revenge. As in Bosnia, such resentment
seeps into the roots of society. Private histories of despair over-
whelm the present. Each generation is raised to exact revenge
for the injustices visited on the last, real or imagined.

"Tell the man what you want to be," said Hyam Temraz to
her two-year-old son, Abed, as she peeped out of the slit of a
black veil one afternoon in Gaza.

"A martyr," the child told me.

"We were in Jordan when my son Baraa was four," she said.
"He saw a Jordanian soldier and ran and hugged him. He asked
him if it was he who would liberate Palestine. He has always
told me that he would be a martyr and that one day I would dig
his grave."

Nezar Rayyan, her husband, was a theology professor at
Islamic University in Gaza. He was a large man with a thick
black beard and the quiet, soft-spoken manner of someone
who has spent much of his life reading. On the walls of his
office, black and white photographs illustrated the history of
Palestinians over the last five decades. They showed lines of
trucks carrying refugees from their villages in 1948, after the
United Nations created Israel and its Arab neighbors attacked
the new state. They showed the hovels of new refugee camps
built after the 1967 war. And they showed the gutted remains of
Palestinian villages in what is now Israel.

Rayyan's grandfather and great-uncle were killed in the 1948 war. His grandmother died shortly after she and her son, Rayyan's father, were forced from their village. His father was passed among relatives and grew up with the bitterness of the dispossessed—a bitterness the father passed on to the son and the son has passed on to the grandchildren.

"There was not a single night that we did not think and talk about Palestine," Rayyan said, his eyes growing moist. "We were taught that our lives must be devoted to reclaiming our land."

Rayyan spent twelve years in an Israeli jail. His brother-in-law blew himself up in a suicide-bomb attack on an Israeli bus in 1998. One of his brothers had been shot dead by Israelis in street protests five years earlier. Another brother was expelled to Lebanon and several more were wounded in clashes.

He gave two of his sons—ages fifteen and sixteen—money to join the youths who throw rocks at Israeli checkpoints. His youngest, Mohammed, twelve, was crippled by an Israeli bullet. All three, according to their father, strive to be one thing: martyrs for Palestine.

"I pray only that God will choose them," he said.

The rewriting and distortion of history—as in all wartime regimes—is crucial. Many of those who went on to prosecute the war in the Balkans, such as the Bosnian Serb leader Radovan Karadžić, who fancied himself a poet, and Croatian president Franjo Tudjman, who after a lifetime in the Yugoslav army began writing nationalist tracts about Croatia, looked at themselves as academics or intellectuals. They believed they were unearthing or championing a true version of history, but what they were doing was tearing down one national identity and replacing it with another. For Tudjman and his Serbian counterparts, the new identity glorified Croatian or Serbian cultural heritage and denigrated the heritage of others. And, for all my sympathy for the plight of the Palestinians, most Palestinians have done the same thing.

Tudjman was part of a long line of mediocre writers and artists who found their voice and a route to power in national chauvinism. In 1963, after a career as an army general, he managed to be appointed professor of history at Zagreb University, even though he lacked a doctoral degree and his dissertation was rejected. He was part of the nationalist campaign for the linguistic separation of the Serbo-Croatian language, which had also been championed by the Nazi puppet state in Croatia run by the Ustashe. His turgid nationalist historical tracts were in the service of one idea—Croatian nationalism. In his book *Impasses of Historical Reality*, he challenged the numbers of victims of World War II genocide by the Germans and the Ustashe. He reduced the number of Jews killed in the Holocaust to one million instead of six million—as well as the number killed in Croatia's main death camp, at Jasenovac, from more than 500,000 to 59,639.

"A Jew is still a Jew," he wrote, "even in the camps they retained their bad characteristics: selfishness, perfidy, meanness, slyness and treachery."

During the 1990 election campaign that saw him ascend to the presidency and lead Croatia's bloody secession from Yugoslavia, he said, "Thank God, my wife is neither a Serb nor a Jew."

In 1992, he said his comments in his books had been "misinterpreted" and in 1994 he offered "an apology" in a letter to B'nai B'rith, saying that he intended to delete "controversial portions" from later editions, which he did. But by then the Croatian state, which carried out the forced expulsion of nearly all the ethnic Serbs—there were 600,000 of them, 12 percent of the population—was complete. Croatia had become the most ethnically cleansed state in the former Yugoslavia.

Tudjman declared Croatia "the national state of the Croatian nation" when he assumed power. And when his government began wholesale dismissals of Serbs from civil service jobs, Serbian communities began arming themselves. The civil society broke down. As Michael Ignatieff wrote in *The Warrior's Honor: Ethnic War and the Modern Conscience*, it is this fear of the other, perhaps more than anything else, that triggers war.

> It is fear that turns minor difference into major, that makes the gulf between ethnicities into a distinction between species, between human and inhuman. And not just fear, but guilt as well. For if you have shared a common life with another group and then suddenly begin to fear them, because they suddenly have power over you, you have to overcome the weight of happy memory; you have to project onto *them* the blame for destroying a common life.[1]

The fervent drive for "authenticity" leads nationalist leaders to use a variety of disciplines to promote and legitimize the cause. In Israel the mania for archeology, for excavating ancient Jewish ruins, is a way of legitimizing the presence of Jews in what was once Palestine. These sites are given a prominence out of proportion to the multitude of other ruins that are not Jewish in character. Sociologists, historians, and writers all seek to find that within the culture that champions the myth and the state, ignoring that which challenges their own supremacy.

No nation is free from this distortion. After the September attacks in the United States a document entitled "Defending Civilization" was compiled by a conservative organization called the American Council of Trustees and Alumni. It set out to show that the American universities did not respond to the September attacks with a proper degree of "anger, patriotism, and support of military intervention." The report offered a list of 115 subversive remarks taken from college newspapers or made on college campuses.

What is at work in this report is the reduction of language to code. Clichés, coined by the state, become the only acceptable vocabulary. Everyone knows what to say and how to respond. It is scripted. Vocabulary shrinks so that the tyranny of nationalist rhetoric leaves people sputtering state-sanctioned slogans. There is a scene in *Othello* when Othello is so consumed by jealousy and rage that he has lost the eloquence and poetry that won him Desdemona. He turns to the audience in Act IV and mutters, "Goats and monkeys!"[2] Nationalist cant, to me, always ends up sounding just as absurd.

The destruction of culture in wartime is also physical. There is an effort to eradicate the monuments and buildings that challenge the myth of the nation. There are thousands of Armenian villages in Turkey, Kurdish villages in Iraq, and Palestinian villages in Israel that have been razed in this process of state-sponsored forgetting. Along with their destruction has been a ferocious campaign to deny the displaced the right to remember where they once belonged.

Those displaced from their homes, those who have seen an assault on their culture, nurture an anger and alienation they assiduously pass on to their children. In many Palestinian refugee camps in Gaza the camps are divided according to villages left behind in 1948. Many of these villages no longer exist. Most of those in the camps never lived in these villages. Yet when you ask where someone is from, the name of the village is the first thing out of his or her mouth. Each side creates a narrative. Each side insists they are the true victims. And each side works overtime to bend their culture to support this narrative.

The city of Mostar in Bosnia was the scene of some of the most savage fighting of the war. The eastern Muslim section was surrounded and heavily shelled by the Bosnian Croats. The town owed its name, "Bridge-keeper," to an elegant, arched Ottoman bridge built in 1566 to join the banks of the Neretva River. The city, a quaint example of Ottoman architecture, was dotted with cobblestone alleys, stone houses, spindly minarets, the Catholic campanile, and Orthodox steeples.

But Croatian commanders, intent on wiping out what was the heart of the city, blasted the bridge for two days in November 1993 until it tumbled into the river. It, like the Moorish-revival library in Sarajevo, which was bombarded for three days by Serbian incendiary bombs in the summer of 1992, was a cultural symbol that did not fit with the narrative of Serbian or Croatian nationalists. It was part of the assault against all cultural icons that spoke of the plurality of peoples in Mostar and Sarajevo.

War, just as it tears down old monuments, demands new ones. These new monuments glorify the state's uniform and unwavering call for self-sacrifice and ultimately self-annihilation. Those who find meaning in the particular, who embrace affirmation not through the collective of the nation but through the love of another individual regardless of ethnic or national identity, are dangerous to the emotional and physical domination demanded by the state. Only one message is acceptable.

A soldier who is able to see the humanity of the enemy makes a troubled and ineffective killer. To achieve corporate action, self-awareness and especially self-criticism must be obliterated. We must be transformed into agents of a divinely inspired will, as defined by the state, just as those we fight must be transformed into the personification of unmitigated evil. There is little room for individuality in war.

The effectiveness of the myths peddled in war is powerful. We often come to doubt own perceptions. We hide these doubts, like troubled believers, sure that no one else feels them. We feel guilty. The myths have determined not only how we should speak but how we should think. The doubts we carry, the scenes we see that do not conform to the myth are hazy, difficult to express, unsettling. And as the atrocities mount, as civil liberties are stripped away (something, with the "War on Terror," already happening to hundreds of thousands of immigrants in the United States), we struggle uncomfortably with the jargon and clichés. But we have trouble expressing our discomfort because the collective shout has made it hard for us to give words to our thoughts.

This self-doubt is aided by the monstrosity of war. We gape and wonder at the collapsing towers of the World Trade Center. They crumble before us, and yet we cannot quite comprehend it. What, really, did we see? In wartime an attack on a village where women and children are killed, an attack that does not conform to the myth peddled by our side, is hard to fathom and articulate. We live in wartime with a permanent discomfort, for in wartime we see things so grotesque and fantastic that they seem beyond human comprehension. War turns human reality into a bizarre carnival that does not seem part of our experience. It knocks us off balance.

On a chilly, rainy day in March 1998 I was in a small Albanian village in Kosovo, twenty-five miles west of the provincial cap-

ital of Pristina. I was waiting with a few thousand Kosovar
Albanian mourners for a red Mercedes truck to rumble down
the dirt road and unload a cargo of fourteen bodies. A group of
distraught women, seated on wooden planks set up on concrete
blocks, was in the dirt yard.

When the truck pulled into the yard I climbed into the back.
Before each corpse, wrapped in bloodstained blankets and rugs,
was lifted out for washing and burial I checked to see if the
body was mutilated. I pulled back the cloth to uncover the faces.
The gouged-out eyes, the shattered skulls, the gaping rows of
broken teeth, and the sinewy strands of flayed flesh greeted me.
When I could not see clearly in the fading light I flicked on my
Maglite. I jotted each disfigurement in my notebook.

The bodies were passed silently out of the truck. They were
laid on crude wooden coffin lids placed on the floor of the
shed. The corpses were wound in white shrouds by a Muslim
cleric in a red turban. The shed was lit by a lone kerosene lamp.
It threw out a ghastly, uneven, yellowish light. In the hasty effort
to confer some dignity on the dead, family members, often
weeping, tried to wash away the bloodstains from the faces.
Most could not do it and had to be helped away.

It was not an uncommon event for me. I have seen many
such dead. Several weeks later it would be worse. I would be in
a warehouse with fifty-one bodies, including children, even
infants, women, and the elderly from the town of Prekaz. I had
spent time with many of them. I stared into their lifeless faces. I
was again in the twilight zone of war. I could not wholly believe
what I saw in front of me.

This sense that we cannot trust what we see in wartime
spreads throughout the society. The lies about the past, the
eradication of cultural, historical, and religious monuments that

have been part of a landscape for centuries, all serve to shift the ground under which we stand. We lose our grip. Whole worlds vanish or change in ways we can not fully comprehend. A catastrophic terrorist strike will have the same effect.

In Bosnia the Serbs, desperately trying to deny the Muslim character of Bosnia, dynamited or plowed over libraries, museums, universities, historic monuments, and cemeteries, but most of all mosques. The Serbs, like the Croats, also got rid of monuments built to honor their own Serb or Croat heroes during the communist era. These monuments championed another narrative, a narrative of unity among ethnic groups that ran contrary to the notion of ancient ethnic hatreds. The partisan monuments that honored Serb and Croat fighters against the Nazis honored, in the new narrative, the wrong Serbs and Croats. For this they had to be erased.

This physical eradication, coupled with intolerance toward any artistic endeavor that does not champion the myth, formed a new identity. The Serbs, standing in flattened mud fields, were able to deny that there were ever churches or mosques on the spot because they had been removed. The town of Zvornik in Serb-held Bosnia once had a dozen mosques. The 1991 census listed 60 percent of its residents as Muslim Slavs. By the end of the war the town was 100 percent Serb. Branko Grujić, the Serb-appointed mayor, informed us: "There never were any mosques in Zvornik."

No doubt he did not believe it. He knew that there had been mosques in Zvornik. But his children and grandchildren would come to be taught the lie. Serbs leaders would turn it into accepted historical fact. There are no shortage of villages in Russia or Germany or Poland where all memory of the Jewish community is gone because the physical culture has been destroyed.

And, when mixed with the strange nightmarish quality of war, it is hard to be completely sure of your own memories.

The destruction of culture sees the state or the group prosecuting the war take control of the two most important mediums that transmit information to the nation—the media and the schools. The alleged "war crimes" of the enemy, real and imagined, are played and replayed night after night, rousing a nation to fury. In the Middle East and the Balkans, along with many othre parts of the world, children are taught to hate. In Egypt pupils are told Jews are interlopers on Arab land. Israel does not appear on schoolroom maps. In Jordan, children learn that Christians are "infidels" who "must be forced into submission," that the Jewish Torah is "perverted," and that Jews have only "their own evil practices" to blame for the Holocaust. Syrian schoolbooks exhort students to "holy war" and paint pictures of Israelis "perpetrating beastly crimes and horrendous massacres," burying people alive in battle and dancing drunk in Islamic holy places in Jerusalem. And Israel, despite efforts in secular state schools to present a more balanced view of Arab history, allows state-funded religious schools to preach that Jewish rule should extend from the Nile in Egypt to the Euphrates in Iraq and that the kingdom of Jordan is occupied Jewish land.[3]

The reinterpretation of history and culture is dizzying and dangerous. But it is the bedrock of the hatred and intolerance that leads to war.

On June 28, 1914, Gavrilo Princip shot and killed Archduke Franz Ferdinand of Austria in a Sarajevo street, an act that set off World War I. But what that makes him in Bosnia depends on which lesson plan you pick up.

"A hero and a poet," says a textbook handed to high school students in the Serb-controlled region of this divided country.

An "assassin trained and instructed by the Serbs to commit this act of terrorism," says a text written for Croatian students. "A nationalist whose deed sparked anti-Serbian rioting that was only stopped by the police from all three ethnic groups," reads the Muslim version of the event.

In communist Yugoslavia, Princip was a hero. But with the partition of Bosnia along ethnic lines, huge swathes of history are reinterpreted. The Muslim books, for example, portray the Ottoman Empire's rule over Bosnia, which lasted 500 years, as a golden age of enlightenment; the Serbs and Croats condemn it as an age of "brutal occupation."

These texts have at least one thing in common: a distaste for Tito, the Communist leader who ruled the country from 1945 to 1980 and was a staunch opponent of the nationalist movements that now hold power. And Tito's state pioneered the replacement of history with myth, forcing schoolchildren to memorize mythical stories about Tito's life and aphorisms.

By the time today's books in the Balkans reach recent history, the divergence takes on ludicrous proportions; each side blames the others for the Bosnian war and makes no reference to crimes or mistakes committed by its own leaders or fighters.

The Muslims are taught that the Serbs "attacked our country" and started the war. The Serbs are told that "Muslims, with the help of mujahadeen fighters from Pakistan, Iraq and Iran, launched a campaign of genocide against the Serbs that almost succeeded."

The Croatian students learn that Croatian forces in "the homeland war" fought off "Serbian and Muslim aggressors."

Even the classics get twisted into a political diatribe. I saw a pro-Milošević production of *Hamlet* in Belgrade that was scripted to convey the message that usurping authority, even illegitimate authority, only brings chaos and ruin. Hamlet was portrayed as a bold and decisive man, constantly training for battle. He was not consumed by questions about the meaning of existence or a desire to withdraw from society, but the steely drive to seize power, even if it plunged the kingdom into chaos. Horatio, usually portrayed as a thoughtful and humane scholar, was the incarnation of evil.

Hamlet's treachery was illustrated at the conclusion of the play when Prince Fortinbras of Norway entered Elsinore to view the carnage. Fortinbras, dressed to look like the chief European representative at the time in Bosnia, Carl Bildt, walked onstage with a Nazi marching song as his entrance music. He unfolded maps showing how, with the collapse of authority, he had now carved up Serbian territory among foreign powers.

"Here is a *Hamlet* for our time," the director, Dejan Krstović, told me. "We want to show audiences what happens when individuals tamper with power and refuse to sublimate their own ambitions for the benefit of the community.

"Because of Hamlet, the bodies pile up on the altar of authority and the system collapses. Because of Hamlet, the foreign prince, Fortinbras, who for us represents the new world order, comes in from the outside and seizes control, as has happened to the Serbs throughout their history."

Every reporter struggles with how malleable and inaccurate memory can be when faced with trauma or stress. Witnesses to war, even moments after a killing or an atrocity, often cannot remember what took place in front of them. They struggle to connect disparate images. And those who see events with some coherency find there is an irreversible pull to twist the facts to conform to the myth. Truth, in such moments, is too nuanced and contradictory for most to swallow. It is best left untouched.

I went one rainy afternoon to the Imperial War Museum in Vienna, mostly to see the rooms dedicated to the 1878 Bosnian rebellion and the assassination of Archduke Franz Ferdinand. His car, peppered with bullet holes, and the bloodstained couch on which he died are on display. But I also wandered through the other rooms designed to honor the bloodlust and forgotten skirmishes of the Austro-Hungarian Empire. When I finished with the World War I exhibit I looked for the room dedicated to World War II. There wasn't one. And when I inquired at the desk, I was told there was no such exhibit in the city. World War II, at least in terms of the collective memory of the Austrian nation, unlike in Germany, might as well have not existed. Indeed, in one of the great European perversions of memory, many Austrians had come to think of themselves as victims of that war.

The destruction of culture plays a crucial role in the solidification of a wartime narrative. When the visible and tangible symbols of one's past are destroyed or denied, the past can be recreated to fit the myth. It is left only to those on the margins to keep the flame of introspection alive, although the destruction of culture is often so great that full recovery is impossible. Yugoslavia, a country that had a vibrant theater and cinema, has seen its cultural life wither, with many of its best talents living in exile or drinking themselves to death in bars in Belgrade or Vienna.

Most societies never recover from the self-inflicted wounds made to their own culture during wartime. War leaves behind not memory but amnesia. Once wars end, people reach back to the time before the catastrophe. The books, plays, cinema take up the established cultural topics; authors and themes are often based on issues and ideas that predated the war. In post-war Germany it was as if Weimar had never ended, as if the war was just some bad, horrible dream from which everyone had just awoken and no one wanted to discuss.

This is why the wall of names that is the Vietnam Veterans Memorial is so important. It was not a project funded or organized by the state but by those who survived and insisted we not forget. It was part of America's battle back to truth, part of our desire for forgiveness. It ultimately held out to us as a nation the opportunity for redemption, although the state has prodded us back towards the triumphalism that led us into Vietnam.

But just as the oppressors engage in selective memory and myth, so do the victims, building unassailable monuments to their own suffering. It becomes impossible to examine, to dispute, or to criticize the myths that have grown up around past suffering of nearly all in war. The oppressors are painted by the survivors as monsters, the victims paint themselves as holy innocents. The oppressors work hard to bury inconvenient facts and brand all in wartime with the pitch of atrocity. They strive to reduce victims to their moral level. Each side creates its own narrative. Neither is fully true.

Until there is a common vocabulary and a shared historical memory there is no peace in any society, only an absence of war. The fighting may have stopped in Bosnia or Cyprus but this does not mean the war is over. The search for a common narrative must, at times, be forced upon a society. Few societies seem able to do this willingly. The temptation, as with the Turks and the Armenian genocide, is to forget or ignore, to wallow in the lie. But reconciliation, self-awareness, and finally the humility that makes peace possible come only when culture no longer serves a cause or a myth but the most precious and elusive of all human narratives—truth.

4

THE SEDUCTION OF BATTLE AND THE PERVERSION OF WAR

Let me have a war, say I: It exceeds peace as far as day
Does night; it's spritely, waking, audible, full of vent.
Peace is a very apoplexy, lethargy, mull'd, deaf, sleepy,
Insensible; a getter of more bastard children than war is a
Destroyer of men.

•

WILLIAM SHAKESPEARE
Coriolanus, Act IV, SCENE V

THE MYTH OF WAR ENTICES US WITH THE ALLURE OF heroism. But the images of war handed to us, even when they are graphic, leave out the one essential element of war—fear. There is, until the actual moment of confrontation, no cost to imagining glory. The visual and audio effects of films, the battlefield descriptions in books, make the experience appear real. In fact the experience is sterile. We are safe. We do not smell rotting flesh, hear the cries of agony, or see before us blood and entrails seeping out of bodies. We view, from a distance, the rush, the excitement, but feel none of the awful gut-wrenching anxiety and humiliation that come with mortal danger. It takes the experience of fear and the chaos of battle, the deafening and disturbing noise, to wake us up, to make us realize that we are not who we imagined we were, that war as displayed by the entertainment industry might, in most cases, as well be ballet. But even with this I have seen soldiers in war try to recreate the fiction of war, especially when a television camera is around to record the attempted heroics. The result is usually pathetic.

The prospect of war is exciting. Many young men, schooled in the notion that war is the ultimate definition of manhood, that only in war will they be tested and proven, that they can discover their worth as human beings in battle, willingly join the great enterprise. The admiration of the crowd, the high-blown rhetoric, the chance to achieve the glory of the previous generation, the ideal of nobility beckon us forward. And people, ironically, enjoy righteous indignation and an object upon which to unleash their anger. War usually starts with collective euphoria.

It is all the more startling that such fantasy is believed, given the impersonal slaughter of modern industrial warfare. I saw high explosives fired from huge distances in the Gulf War reduce battalions of Iraqis to scattered corpses. Iraqi soldiers were nothing more on the screens of sophisticated artillery pieces than little dots scurrying around like ants—that is, until they were blasted away. Bombers dumped tons of iron fragmentation bombs on them. Our tanks, which could outdistance their Soviet-built counterparts, blew Iraqi armored units to a standstill. Helicopters hovered above units like angels of death in the sky. Here there was no pillage, no warlords, no collapse of unit discipline, but the cold and brutal efficiency of industrial warfare waged by well-trained and highly organized professional soldiers. It was a potent reminder why most European states and America live in such opulence and determine the fate of so many others. We equip and train the most efficient killers on the planet.

I drove my Land Rover down the highway north of Kuwait City a day or two following the liberation. For seven miles there was a line of burned-out cars, trucks, and tanks, many with the charred remains of Iraqi soldiers inside. The retreating convoy had been strafed by F-16 fighter jets. Some of the 1,500 vehicles were turned in an apparent attempt to flee back towards the city. They had caused a massive traffic jam. The only escape was on foot. The air was pungent with the stench of rotting bodies. In the cab of one truck were the blackened remains of a soldier curled up over the steering wheel. Bits of legs and arms stuck out in strange positions from the burned metal. Cobra helicopters hovered noisily above me.

Millions of men watched mass death in World War I. They understood the power of modern weaponry. They struggled after the war to fit back into European society. But the world, from World War I onward, had changed. Writers such as Joseph Roth or Ernst Jünger understood that we had entered into a new era, one in which we would always flirt with death and self-destruction on a hitherto unknown scale. Redemption, since World War I, comes to us only through apocalypse. The old world order, captured in works such as the 1937 French film *Grand Illusion*, died with the end of the spontaneous 1914 Christmas truce. The accepted principles of humanity, the archaic code of the warrior, became quaint and obsolete. The technological and depersonalized levels of organized killing begun in World War I have defined warfare ever since.

"Having torn out of its midst millions upon millions of its

own people, inverted and perverted every value and belief, exploited to the limit humanity's willingness to sacrifice itself for a higher cause in order to perpetuate the most heinous crimes, the war has left us with a legacy of gaping absences of memory and identity, culture and biography," wrote the Israeli historian Omer Bartov.[1]

But even in the new age of warfare we cling to the outdated notion of the single hero able to carry out daring feats of courage on the battlefield. Such heroism is about as relevant as mounting bayonet or cavalry charges. But peddling the myth of heroism is essential, maybe even more so now, to entice soldiers into war. Men in modern warfare are in service to technology. Many combat veterans never actually see the people they are firing at nor those firing at them, and this is true even in low-intensity insurgencies.

To be sure, soldiers who kill innocents pay a tremendous personal emotional and spiritual price. But within the universe of total war, equipped with weapons that can kill hundreds or thousands of people in seconds, soldiers only have time to reflect later. By then these soldiers often have been discarded, left as broken men in a civilian society that does not understand them and does not want to understand them. Once violence on this scale is unleashed it usually continues to plague societies. The civil war in El Salvador, as in many African states, has left the country beset by violent crime and dominated by armed militias and gangs. We are hostage to a vast and powerful military-industrial complex that exports more weapons than all other nations combined.

I knew a Muslim soldier, a father, who fought on the front lines around Sarajveo. His unit, in one of the rare attempts to take back a few streets controlled by the Serbs, pushed across

Serb lines. They did not get very far. The fighting was intense. As he moved down the street he heard a door swing open. He fired a burst from his AK-47 assault rifle. A twelve-year-old girl dropped dead. He saw in the body of the unknown girl lying prostrate in front of him the image of his own twelve-year-old daughter. He broke down. He had to be helped back to the city. He was lost for the rest of the war, shuttered inside his apartment, nervous, morose, and broken. This experience is far more typical of warfare than the Rambo heroics we are fed by the state and the entertainment industry. The cost of killing is all the more bitter because of the deep disillusionment that war usually brings.

It takes little in wartime to turn ordinary men into killers. Most give themselves willingly to the seduction of unlimited power to destroy and all feel the heavy weight of peer pressure. Few, once in battle, can find the strength to resist.

The German veteran of World War I Erich Maria Remarque, in *All Quiet on the Western Front,* wrote of the narcotic of war that quickly transformed men into beasts. He knew the ecstatic high of violence and the debilitating mental and physical destruction that comes with prolonged exposure to war's addiction.

"We run on," he wrote, "overwhelmed by this wave that bears us along, that fills us with ferocity, turns us into thugs, into murderers, into God knows what devils; this wave that multiplies our strength with fear and madness and greed of life, seeking and fighting for nothing but our deliverance."[2]

The historian Christopher Browning noted the willingness to kill in *Ordinary Men,* his study of Reserve Police Battalion 101 in Poland during World War II. The battalion was ordered to shoot 1,800 Jews in the Polish village of Jozefow in a day-long action. The men in the unit had to round up the Jews, march them into the forest, and one by one order them to lie down in a row. The victims, including women, infants, children, and the elderly, were shot dead at close range.

The battalion was ordered to do the killing on the morning of July 12, 1942. They were offered the option to refuse, an option only about a dozen men took, although more asked to be relieved once the killing began. Those who did not want to continue, Browning says, were disgusted rather than plagued by conscience. When the men returned to the barracks they "were depressed, angered, embittered and shaken."[3] They drank heavily. They were told not to talk about the event, "but they needed no encouragement in that direction."[4]

In the massacres that followed, the killings by the battalion became less personal. The executioners drank now, as executioners did in Bosnia and Kosovo, before their work. Having killed once, Browning wrote, the men "did not experience such a traumatic shock the second time."[5] It no longer became hard to find volunteers, and the killing escalated. In a massacre that became known as the "Harvest Festival" some 500 men killed 30,500 Jewish inhabitants of the work camps Trawniki, Poniatowa, and Majdanek in a matter of days.

The men in the battalion, aged thirty-seven to forty-two, were not elite troops. They were not highly trained nor had they been specially picked for the job. They were of middle- or lower-class origin. And their behavior, given the savagery of modern warfare, has been widely replicated. There are no shortages of former soldiers and militiamen in Algeria, Argentina, Rwanda, El Salvador, Iraq, or Bosnia who have done the same. There are always people willing to commit unspeakable human atrocity in exchange for a little power and privilege.

The task of carrying out violence, of killing, leads to perversion. The seductiveness of violence, the fascination with the grotesque—the Bible calls it "the lust of the eye"—the god-like empowerment over other human lives and the drug of war combine, like the ecstasy of erotic love, to let our senses command our bodies. Killing unleashes within us dark undercurrents that see us desecrate and whip ourselves into greater orgies of destruction. The dead, treated with respect in peacetime, are abused in wartime. They become pieces of performance art. Corpses were impaled in Bosnia on the sides of barn doors, decapitated, or draped like discarded clothing over fences. They were dumped into rivers, burned alive in homes, herded into warehouses and shot and mutilated, or left on roadsides. Children could pass them on the street, gape at them and walk on.

There are few anti-war movies or novels that successfully portray war, for amidst the horror is also the seduction of the machine of war, all-powerful, all-absorbing. Most of the effective anti-war novels—such as Elsa Morante's *History: A Novel*—focus on the effects of war, on those who bear the brunt of war's brutality. Morante, who spent a year hiding among remote farming villages south of Rome at the end of World War II, set out to write a novel about those whom history ignores and forgets. Her world was that of victims. It is was a world not of heroics and glory but of rape, bombing raids, crime, cattle cars filled with human beings being taken to slaughter, soldiers dying of frostbite, and the fear of secret police and the military. In her world, no one had control.[6]

Pity is often banished in war. And the desperate struggle of the weak to survive, so fundamental to what war is about, rarely seems able to achieve the centrality it deserves.

Following the Gulf War, during the Shiite uprising in Basra,

I was captured by the Iraqi Republican Guard. The soldiers threw me onto the floor in the back of my jeep, pressed the barrel of an AK–47 assault rifle to my forehead, and drove into the desert. They stripped me of my M–65 jacket, useful to them in the cold desert night. In the pocket were three books: *Antony and Cleopatra*, *The Iliad*, and Joseph Conrad's *Outcast of the Islands*. I was bereft of reading material, left to cling to those lines of Shakespeare and poems by W. H. Auden, T. S. Eliot, and William Butler Yeats I had memorized in my youth. Over and over during my captivity I pieced them back together, phrase by phrase, line by line, resurrecting passages uttered over a decade before as a student actor, along with poems that constant repetition had made a part of me.

In the misery of the fighting—our small convoy was heavily ambushed on the second day, sixty miles north of Basra—and gnawing uncertainty, these passages at once consoled, pained, and protected me, often from myself.

One afternoon, in the driving rain, I was seated in a Pajero jeep, hot-wired and stolen by my Iraqi captors during the frantic flight from Kuwait City. We had stopped to fill our canteens from muddy puddles. All of the water purification plants had been bombed. The muck and rainwater had already turned my own guts inside out. As I made my way to the brackish pools I noticed a woman and two small children scooping up their hands to drink. I knew what such foul water would do to these innocents and in the cold downpour recited Auden's "Epitaph on a Tyrant" as a kind of quiet, unintelligible blessing:

Perfection, of a kind, was what he was after,
And the poetry he invented was easy to understand;
He knew human folly like the back of his hand,
And was greatly interested in armies and fleets;

When he laughed, respectable senators burst with laughter,
And when he cried the little children died in the streets.[7]

As the days wore on, sick, with little to eat, constantly under fire (at one point for sixteen hours), I began to fully appreciate the misery, pathos, and courage of professional soldiership.

One night, sheltering from rebel snipers behind an armored personnel carrier, some of my guards and I shared one can of peas and a jar of peach jam. Each of us got a few peas dropped into our dirt-caked palms and one plastic spoonful of jam. It was all any of us ate that day.

All great works of art find their full force in those moments when the conventions of the world are stripped away and confront our weakness, vulnerability, and mortality. For learning, in the end, meant little to writers like Shakespeare unless it translated into human experience.

"As long as reading is for us the instigator whose magic keys have opened the door to those dwelling-places deep within us that we would not have known how to enter, its role in our lives is salutary," Proust wrote. "It becomes dangerous, on the other hand, when, instead of awakening us to the personal life of the mind, reading tends to take its place."[8]

But when we write about warfare the prurient fascination usually rises up to defeat the message. The successful anti-war novels and films are those, like Elsa Morante's, that eschew battle scenes and focus on the heartbreak of violence and slaughter. It no doubt helped that Elsa Morante was a woman, less able to identify with and be seduced by war and the allure of violence. But in most wars women, if not engaged in the fighting, stand on the sidelines to cheer their men onward. Few are immune.

One of the most widely read works of Holocaust literature

in Israel is not the quiet, meditative reflections of writers such as Primo Levi, who struggled to understand the capacity for evil in all of us, but Ka'Tzetnik's six autobiographic volumes, published in the 1950s. What troubles the Israeli historian Omer Bartov is that what "makes them so gripping: namely, their obsession with violence and perversity."[9]

The main character of Ka'Tzetnik's sextet, *House of Dolls*, is a young woman who is made into a prostitute for German soldiers.[10] The books were reissued in 1994 and handed out by the Israeli Ministry of Education as recommended reading on the Holocaust in high schools.

"Nothing could be a greater taboo than deriving sexual pleasure from the fact that the central sites for these actions were the concentration camps," Bartov writes. "Nothing could be a greater taboo than deriving sexual pleasure from pornography in the context of the Holocaust; hence nothing could be as exciting. That Israeli youth learned about sex and perversity, and derived sexual gratification, from books describing the manner in which Nazis tortured Jews, is all the more disturbing, considering that we are speaking about a society whose population consisted of a large proportion of Holocaust survivors and their offspring."[11]

The effects on society can only be guessed, he argues, but there is little doubt that those subsequent generations "have not been wholly liberated from this pernicious trap, whereby they must have more of the violent and ruthless attributes associated with the perpetrators so as not to become their victims (whom on some level of consciousness they are still defending)."[12]

The conflict between the Israelis and the Palestinians has left each side embracing death. They each believe that they are the only real victims. There is a celebration of suicidal martyrdom and justification of the tit-for-tat killing of noncombatants.

On a recent trip to the region, I visited the Khan Younis refugee camp in the Gaza Strip. As the searing afternoon heat and swirling eddies of dust enveloped the camp, I sought cover, slumping under the shade of a palm-roofed hut on the edge of the dunes. I was momentarily defeated by the grit that covered my face and hair, the jostling crowds, the stench of the open sewers and rotting garbage.

Barefoot boys, clutching ragged soccer balls and kites made out of scraps of paper, squatted a few feet away under scrub trees. Men, in flowing white or gray *galabias*—homespun robes—smoked cigarettes outside their doorways. They fingered prayer beads and spoke in hushed tones as they boiled tea or coffee on sooty coals in small iron braziers in the shade of the eaves. Two emaciated donkeys, their ribs outlined on their flanks, were tethered to wooden carts with rubber wheels.

It was still. The camp waited, as if holding its breath. And then, out of the dry furnace air a disembodied voice crackled over a loudspeaker from the Israeli side of the camp's perimeter fence.

"Come on, dogs," the voice boomed in Arabic. "Where are all the dogs of Khan Younis? Come! Come!"

I stood up and walked outside the hut. The invective spewed out in a bitter torrent. "Son of a bitch!" "Son of a whore!" "Your mother's cunt!"

The boys darted in small packs up the sloping dunes to the electric fence that separated the camp from the Jewish settlement abutting it. They lobbed rocks towards a jeep, mounted with a loudspeaker and protected by bulletproof armor plates and metal grating, that sat parked on the top of a hill known as Gani Tal. The soldier inside the jeep ridiculed and derided them. Three ambulances—which had pulled up in anticipation of what was to come—lined the road below the dunes.

There was the boom of a percussion grenade. The boys, most no more than ten or eleven years old, scattered, running clumsily through the heavy sand. They descended out of sight behind the dune in front of me. There were no sounds of gunfire. The soldiers shot with silencers. The bullets from M–16 rifles, unseen by me, tumbled end-over-end through their slight bodies. I would see the destruction, the way their stomachs were ripped out, the gaping holes in their limbs and torsos, later in the hospital.

I had seen children shot in other conflicts I have covered—death squads gunned them down in El Salvador and Guatemala, mothers with infants were lined up and massacred in Algeria, and Serb snipers put children in their sights and watched them crumple onto the pavement in Sarajevo—but I had never watched soldiers entice children like mice into a trap and murder them for sport.

All wars feed off martyrs, the mention of the dead instantly shutting down all arguments for compromise or tolerance for the other. It is the dead who rule. They speak from beyond the grave urging a nation onward to revenge.

Murad Abdel Rahman, thirty-seven, stared vacantly in front of him, mechanically standing up from one in a long line of purple plastic chairs placed in the street to shake the hands of mourners who greeted him. Posters of his dead eleven-year-old son Ali Murad adorned the walls. Black flags of mourning, green banners with Koranic verses, and signs from Palestinian factions surrounded the white canopy that had been spread out over the rutted, dirt street.

Men, seated in the rows, inclined their heads together to talk. A truck, manned by militants, sat parked. The bearded Islamists in white robes waited to turn the funeral into a piece of propaganda, with the boy's body as a prop.

The father said he had had no part in the decorations, which included posters of Saddam Hussein. He seemed indifferent to the elaborate display. He spoke slowly, his puffy eyes and uncomprehending gaze giving the lie to the rhetoric of sacrifice and glory that the militants would have the world believe marks such occasions.

"This is what I worked so hard to prevent," he said, his voice hoarse and low. "I took Ali with me every day to my restaurant at 6:00 in the morning on al-Bahar Street. I made him promise he would not go to the dunes to throw rocks. Yesterday he asked to go home at 3:00. He said he had to study for the make-up sessions they are holding for all the school closings this year. A half-hour after he left, people came running to tell me he was shot in the leg. I ran through the streets to the hospital. They would not let me in. They said he would be discharged soon. They told me he was OK. I forced my way inside and saw him lying in the corridor dead with a bullet hole in his heart. I fainted."

Several small boys stood glumly at the edge of the tent. They said they had called to Ali as he walked home to join them on the dunes.

"We all threw rocks," said ten-year-old Ahmed Moharb. "Over the loudspeaker the soldier told us to come to the fence to get chocolate and money. Then they cursed us. Then they fired a grenade. We started to run. They shot Ali in the back. I won't go again. I am afraid."

On the Sunday afternoon I witnessed, the Israelis shot four boys or young men, one of whom would die from his wounds the next day.

The residents in the camp, who had time to study the taunt-ing, insisted that the Arabic accent over the loudspeakers was Lebanese. They believed that mercenaries from the South

Lebanese Army, once a Christian proxy army for Israel and long a bitter foe of the Palestinians, had been integrated into the Israeli force. The word in Palestinian Arabic for "shoot"—*ahousak*—was not used over the loudspeakers; in its place I heard the Lebanese word in Arabic—*atoohak*. And the camp residents said they heard Lebanese music coming from the guard posts.

Ali's small body was loaded onto the back of a truck. A cadre of young men, some bearded and in robes, others dressed in black and wearing wraparound sunglasses, marched with automatic weapons pointed in the air in three rows behind the bier. They fired rounds in the air. The crowd of several hundred, egged on by the speakers mounted on the truck, chanted Islamic and anti-Israeli slogans.

"Mothers of Jews!" they shouted. "We will make you weep like Palestinian mothers."

The funerals had added another dimension to the religious life of the camp, one that increased the reach of the Islamic militants. The truck, with a generator in the back and stacks of huge loudspeakers on the cab, lumbered ahead of the procession. It blasted out verses from the Koran, calls to die, and promises of glory for martyrs. Swarms of young boys ran along behind. The crowd passed the graphic murals and graffiti on the walls. One showed an Israeli bus, marked by a Star of David, on fire and smashed from an explosion. "Don't be merciful to those inside" read the slogan underneath. "Blow it up! Hit it!" It was signed "Hamas."

There was a frightening symbiotic relationship between the Israeli soldiers taunting children on the dunes and the Islamic militants who promoted martyrdom. It spun Gaza into an ever faster and more passionate dance with death.

Neamon Mohammed Faid, twenty, pulled up his shirt when I entered his hospital room in Nasser Hospital to reveal a flesh-colored bandage wrapped mummy-like around his torso. He had been shot below the heart. The bullet had spun out of his body in his lower back. Part of his kidney had been removed, along with much of his stomach and his spleen. His father and mother hovered over him.

"Yes, it was on the dunes," he said wearily. "The Jews were saying, 'Your mother is a bitch! Fuck your mother!' And then they would say, 'Come! Come!'"

He was with four others pitching stones at the jeep when the soldiers opened fire. He had been told moments before by the Palestinian police, who watched the daily shootings with resignation, to leave.

In Khan Younis's second hospital, al-Amal, thirteen-year-old Fahdi Abu Ammouna lay on a bed, his feet propped up on a pillow. Patches of dried blood covered the sheets. Late in the afternoon he had been throwing rocks at the jeeps. He said some of the rocks hit the army jeep, a claim I doubted.

"The soldier said over the loudspeaker that those who wanted to live should run," he said, "and those who wanted to die should stay. Then they swore at us. They said everyone who lives in Khan Younis is a dog. I started to run. I was shot. I never heard any shots. The bullet went through both of my legs. I crawled to the ambulance. It was the first time I went."

His mother, seated next to him and wearing a black headscarf, slowly shook her head.

"He goes every day," she said softly. "I sent my older son to bring him home. And he was not home five minutes before he went back. I tell the boys it is useless, throwing stones and becoming a martyr will not make the Israelis leave. My sister has lost a son. My brother has lost a son. One of my uncles was killed and a cousin is dead. I tell them to look at the history of our struggle. All these deaths achieve nothing."

She began to talk about the first uprising, or *intifada*, that had led to the Oslo peace agreement. Her husband, Samir, who stood in a blue shirt, white pants, and sandals at the end of the bed, was at the time a prisoner in Israel. One morning Israeli soldiers burst into her two-room house in the refugee camp while she was baking bread. Fahdi was six months old. They turned the place upside down and threw Fahdi on the stove. He was severely burned. As she spoke she gently placed her fingers on her son's small arm, hooked up to an intravenous tube.

"The children are fed this hatred for the Jews from the day they are born," she said. "All they hear is that we have to get rid of the Jewish enemy. The call to fight is pumped out over the radio and the television. The trucks go through the streets of the camp praising the new martyrs and calling for more. The posters of the martyrs are everywhere. And the kids see their fathers, helpless against the Israelis, out of work, and admire the militants with guns. They want to fight."

The violent breakup of Yugoslavia, which was preceded by economic collapse, began in 1991. It was the same year that the government decided to permit hard-core sex films to be broadcast on public stations and that the first locally made pornographic film was produced. While the old Communist Yugoslavia did not censor love scenes in its state-run film industry, it condemned pornography as the exploitation of women and banned its production. The first graphic pictures of mutilated and dead from the war, along with the racial diatribes against Muslims and Croats, hit the airwaves at the same time Yugoslavs were allowed to watch porno films. The war was, like the sex films, about the lifting of taboos, about new forms of entertainment to mask the economic and political collapse of Yugoslavia. War and sex were the stimulants to divert a society that was collapsing.

The world, as it is in war, had been turned upside down. Those who had worked hard all their lives, put their meager savings into banks, and struggled to live on pensions or salaries, lost everything. The unscrupulous, who had massive debts, never had to repay them, lived off the black market or crime, used force to get what they wanted, and became fabulously rich and powerful. The moral universe disintegrated. There was a new code.

The criminal class, many of whom made their fortunes by plundering the possessions of ethnic Croats and Muslims who were expelled from their homes or killed in Bosnia during the war, had rented apartments where they sold stolen clothes from Italy. Huge outdoor fairs were held where you could buy stolen cars complete with fake registrations. Drugs, protection rackets, prostitution, not to speak of duty-free cigarettes (smuggled into Italy with speedboats from the Montenegrin coast), became the country's major businesses as state-run factories folded. In Belgrade, at the war's height, there were seventy escort services, three adult cinemas, and twenty pornographic magazines. After midnight the public television channels ran hard-core porno films.

Hedonism and perversion spiraled out of control as inflation ate away at the local currency. Those who had worked hard all their lives were now reviled as dupes and fools. They haunted the soup kitchens. The loyalty they had expressed to the state or to the institutions they worked for had left them beggars. They held worthless war bonds. They collected pensions, when they

were paid, that amounted to a few dollars. They sold rugs, tea
sets, china, paintings, anything they could dig out of their apartments at huge open-air flea markets. Their children, no matter
how well educated, worked in menial jobs abroad so they could
mail back enough for their parents to buy food. Distraught
teachers said they struggled to cope with children as young as
eleven who had been exposed to scenes of graphic sado-
masochism on television and copied the sexual acts they witnessed. Domestic violence, often by men who were out of
work or had not received their small salaries for months, was
widespread.

The ancient Greeks linked war and love. Aphrodite, the god-
dess of love and the wife of Hephaestos, the lame blacksmith
who forged the weapons and armor for the gods, became the
mistress of Ares, the god of war. It was an illicit affair. Ares,
impetuous, quarrelsome, and often drunk, was hated among the
gods. He loved battle for its own sake. His sister, Eris, spread
rumor and jealousy to whip up the winds of war. Ares never
favored one city or party against another. He frequently
switched loyalties, abandoning those he had once helped. He
delighted only in slaughter. It was only Eris and Aphrodite, who
had a perverse passion for him, who loved him. Hades honored
him because of the legions of slain young men he dispatched to
the underworld.

There is in wartime a nearly universal preoccupation with
sexual liaisons. There is a kind of breathless abandon in
wartime, and those who in peacetime would lead conservative
and sheltered lives give themselves over to wanton carnal relationships. Men, and especially soldiers, are preoccupied with little else. With power reduced to such a raw level and the
currency of life and death cheap, eroticism races through all
relationships. There is in these encounters a frenetic lust that

seeks, on some level, to replicate or augment the drug of war. It is certainly not about love, indeed love itself in wartime is hard to sustain or establish.

Casual encounters are charged with a raw, high-voltage sexual energy that smacks of the self-destructive lust of war itself. The erotic in war is like the rush of battle. It overwhelms the participants. Women who might not otherwise be hailed as beauties are endowed with the charms of Helen. Men endowed with little more than the power to kill are lionized and desired. Bodies, just as they lie scattered and immobile a few hundred yards away, become tools, objects to an end. The fleeting sexual encounters, intense, overpowering, and largely anonymous, deflate with tremendous speed and leave behind guilt, even disgust, and a void that expands into a swamp of loneliness. Stay long enough in war and real love, real tenderness and connection, becomes nearly impossible. Sex in war is another variant of the drug of war.

"If we are honest," the philosopher J. Glenn Gray wrote in *The Warriors,* "most of us who were civilian soldiers in recent wars will confess that we spent incomparably more time in the service of Eros during our military careers than ever before or again in our lives. When we were in uniform almost any girl who was faintly attractive had an erotic appeal for us. For their part, millions of women find a strong sexual attraction in the military uniform, particularly in time of war."[13]

The Polish journalist Ryszard Kapuściński in *Another Day of Life,* his book about the Angolan civil war, told of a twenty-year-old rebel soldier named Carlotta, a member of the Popular Movement for the Liberation of Angola (MPLA), the insurgent group backed by the Soviet Union and Cuba. A legendary fighter—and Kapuściński correctly pointed out that girls make much better child soldiers than boys because they are less prone to hysterics—she met Kapuściński and his crew in a baggy commando uniform with an automatic slung on her shoulder. The men are besotted. They see her as endowed with "elusive charm" and "great beauty."[14]

"Later when I developed the pictures of her, the only pictures of Carlotta that remained, I saw that she wasn't so beautiful. Yet nobody said as much out loud, so as not to destroy our myth, our image of Carlotta from that October afternoon in Benguela."[15]

"She seemed beautiful. Why?" he asked. "Because that was the kind of mood we were in, because we needed it, because we wanted it that way. We always create the beauty of women, and that day we created Carlotta's beauty. I can't explain it any other way."[16]

Those relationships that appear to extend beyond the erotic, however, are also hollow. Many liaisons in wartime look and feel like love, but they too have more to do with projection than reality. Soldiers fall in love with women across a vast cultural divide, although the linguistic barrier makes communication difficult. Here too war perverts the relationship. For in the soldier lies absolute power, protection, and possibly escape. The woman's appeal lies in the gentleness that is absent in war. Each finds in the other attributes that war wipes out—tenderness or security. But few of these liaisons last once the conflict ends.

The young are drawn to those who wield violence and power. Why study to be a doctor or a lawyer when such academic toil was not rewarded, indeed often considered worthless? Why uphold a common morality, including hard work, when the outcome was destitution? Why have any personal or moral standards when these standards were irrelevant?

The killers and warlords became the object of sexual fantasy.

The paramilitary leader Zeljko Ražnatović, known as Arkan, was, according to Serbian opinion polls, one of the most desired men in the country.

War turned Belgrade, along with every other capital caught up in conflict, into Caligula's Rome. There was a moral lassitude in the air, bred of hopelessness and apathy. The city's best-known gangsters, sometimes in the company of Milošević's son Marko, who threatened bar patrons with automatic weapons, cruised the streets in BMWs and Mercedes. They filled the nightclubs of Belgrade, dressed in their expensive black Italian suits and leather jackets.

At the Lotus, one such club in the downtown area of the city, pulsating music thumped through the blue haze of cigarette smoke and strobe lights. Scantily clad strippers spun around poles and leapt into two huge floodlit animal cages with men and women from the dance floor. The young couples began to peel off their shirts and simulate sex with the dancers.

"Stay a little longer," a patron shouted at me. "The simulation is just the beginning."

Under a spotlight a stripper known as Nina, a star of Belgrade's violent and frenetic nightlife, descended a spiral staircase into the mayhem. Her lover and bodyguard, a stocky woman with closely cropped hair and a German Luger tucked in her belt, followed her menacingly from the shadows. Nina moved seductively around the dance floor bathed in light. She nuzzled up to the patrons.

War breaks down long-established prohibitions against violence, destruction, and murder. And with this often comes the crumbling of sexual, social, and political norms as the domination and brutality of the battlefield is carried into personal life. Rape, mutilation, abuse, and theft are the natural outcome of a world in which force rules, in which human beings are objects. The infection is pervasive. Society in wartime becomes atomized. It rewards personal survival skills and very often leaves those with decency and compassion trampled under the rush. The pride one feels in a life devoted to the nation or to an institution or a career or an ideal is often replaced by shame and guilt. Those who have lived upright, socially productive lives are punished for their gullibility in the new social order.

The wars in the Balkans saw the rise of rape camps, places where women were kept under guard and repeatedly abused by Serbian paramilitary forces. When this became boring—for perverse sex, like killing, must constantly entail the new and bizarre—the women were mutilated and killed, reportedly on video. Women were also held in very similar conditions, and later murdered, in Argentina during the Dirty War. Sexual slaves in Argentina were used and then discarded like waste, their drugged bodies at times dumped from helicopters into the sea.

At dusk in 1992, after being smuggled through Serbian lines ringing Sarajevo in the back of a jeep belonging to the United Nations High Commissioner for Refugees, I was taken to a large school in the Bosnian town of Zenica. There Bosnian Croats, in essence Bosnians who were Catholic, were huddled after being driven from their homes by Arkan's militia. They were some of the 10,000 Muslims and Croats who had been driven from their homes in Bosanski Novi, Sanski Most, and Prijedor over the last four days in one of the periodic waves of ethnic cleansing by the Serbs. As usual, the men of fighting age had been separated and detained. About 5,000 of them were now missing.

The displaced, robbed of every possession and then driven on buses to Muslim front lines, sat on the cement floor. Children wailed. The smell of cigarette smoke and unwashed bodies mingled in the dimly lit rooms. There was no electricity. Kerosene lamps provided a dim light. As I pushed through the crowd, hastily jotting down notes, it became clear that most small villages had lost nearly all their draft-age men. The men had been gathered in town squares and beheaded, beaten to death with sledgehammers, forced to dig their own graves and to watch as their daughters or wives were raped in front of them. I was not surprised.

The women who had been raped were easy to spot: sullen, broken, and uncommunicative. Most did not want to speak of the experience. I learned about it through others. The scene was typical. I looked into the blank, uncomprehending faces of the children and despaired for the next generation.

In town after town in Bosnia and Kosovo, warlords turned universes upside down. They preyed on the weak to fulfill their own carnal lusts and desires. They stole and raped, murdered and abused, and their immoral universe proved ascendant. In village after village in Bosnia, Afghanistan, or the Congo, the killers and their militias ruled. They were once embraced as saviors, shielded by the myth of war, but they had become parasites.

These militias, without the discipline or military code of the professional soldier, were frightening. They were populated with criminals, misfits, and children who drive around with car trunks full of weapons they did not know how to use. They killed and tortured according to whims and moods. They enjoyed turning us into pawns, playing with our fear, holding us as "guests" while they unleashed a lifetime of bitterness upon those around them. Once in a village in Kosovo I found a local warlord from the Kosovo Liberation Army with enough weapons dangling off him to outfit three or four fighters. He began barking orders to his hapless followers and when they did not heed his demands started firing into the dirt. Blood began oozing out of one of his combat boots. Determined not to let his visitors see his self-inflicted wounds he clenched his teeth and limped away. It was among the rabble, the barbarians, that I longed for the Roman cohort, the drilled and organized mass that makes up professional armies.

In wartime nearly everyone becomes an accomplice. The huge dislocations, the millions who lose homes and property, are often compensated with the property of those that were forced out. Those who had their homes taken away from them in Srebrenica by the Bosnian Serbs were later given the homes of Serbs who fled the suburbs of Sarajevo. The moral destructiveness of ethnic cleansing, like the psychic wounds of war, thus reverberates throughout a society. Families who are stripped of all they own and then handed by the state apartments that were seized from others are complicitous, whether they like it or not, in the crimes of war.

These dislocations, a large and usually deliberate part of modern warfare, destroy communal structures and weaken ties to those beyond the immediate ethnic group. They create, as Hannah Arendt pointed out, a population of stateless individuals, refugees within their own countries, who to survive must share in the loot of war.[17] The policies of communist Russia revolved around such internal displacement. Political or moral dissent is silenced, since nearly all are forced to become accomplices. It is hard to condemn ethnic cleansing when you live in someone else's home.

Following the NATO bombing of the Bosnian Serb army in the fall of 1995, I accompanied several thousand Bosnian Muslim soldiers, backed by Croatian artillery, as they drove retreating

Serbs across central Bosnia. We pushed into town after town that had been abandoned often only hours before. The front lines became mixed up and confused, with soldiers from the two armies colliding into each other in messy little gun battles. In those few weeks, an estimated 100,000 Serbs were made homeless. In one village a desperate group of Serbs gunned down a family in a car, stole the vehicle, and fled.

The village of Ključ was a depressing collection of dirty stucco dwellings surrounding a muddy central square. I was there on a rainy September afternoon when five packed buses stopped along the road. Clutching his mother's hand, five-year-old Mirnes Mujaković descended from one of the buses. The boy searched for a place to sit on the sacks of clothing piled up along the street as the cargo was unloaded.

The boy's home, friends, toys, and neighborhood had all vanished eight days earlier in a confusing blur of loud threats, pushing, beatings, tears, and a bewildering night under the trees waiting for a boat to cross the Sava River into the Croatian town of Davor. For a week he and his Muslim neighbors had lived on the bus, shuttled from Croatia to Slovenia and now to Bosnia.

Two elderly people in his group had died. He saw their bodies. And strange, gruff men had handed out brown boxes with tins of food so everyone could eat. Now, a man with a clipboard was sending families off to empty houses, many with furniture, clothes, and the bloated bodies of farm animals lying haphazardly in the yards. The houses had been hastily marked with white numbers on the doors.

"Are you OK?" asked his mother, Rasema, as she pulled a sweatshirt from a bag and slipped it over her son's head. "What do you think?"

The boy did not answer. His mother looked up and offered an explanation.

"You see," she said, her hand shaking as she dabbed a piece of pink cloth below her eyes. "You see, his father went away."

Fathers often went away in this war. And fathers often did not come back. This was not the first Balkan war fought by men with memories like those being forged in Mirnes's mind. But for now, the boy sought only the solace of his mother's arms.

Soon the man with the clipboard came to the mother and son and took them down a dirt track to a small house that had been abandoned a week earlier by a Serb family. I walked with them. The house still had dishes with scraps of food on them, and clothes were strewn on the floor. A Serbian Orthodox icon hung on a wall. And a black and white wedding picture, apparently decades old, was tacked up over the bed.

"We are going to be getting a lot of these families," said Mehmet Makić, the head of the local displaced persons office, as he and I stood in the muddy yard. "The Serbs are pushing all the remaining Muslims around Banja Luka out. They are turning the houses of the Muslims over to the new Serb refugees. We expect to get about 11,000 people soon. The Serbs are taking the Muslim homes. We are putting the Muslims in the Serb homes."

The 300 people who arrived in Ključ on the buses were from the town of Prnjavor. Most had survived more than three years without work since the Serbs took control of their part of Bosnia. Most of them also had endured harassment and beatings and had seen their young men disappear. But in the last week, in the wake of the sweeping advance of the Bosnian Army, the mood got even uglier.

"We paid for this in advance," said thirty-nine-year-old Rifet

Ramović. "The Serb soldiers stood by the buses when we left and demanded that each of us pay them 150 to 300 deutsche marks. People had to beg their neighbors for help so they could afford to get out. By the time we left, most of us had nothing."

In the small living room of her new house, not far from where I had left Mirnes and his mother, Fatima Cura looked around. She and her husband started cleaning up the unfamiliar possessions scattered on the floor.

"I feel guilty," she said. "This is some else's home. Is this right?"

Her husband did not answer as he knelt to pick up pieces of stale bread from the floor.

"We lived twenty-seven years together in our house," she said. "We expected something like this, so we sent our children out."

Their son was in Sweden and their daughter was in a refugee camp in Germany.

"Then one night last week the Serbs came and put a paper on our door saying we no longer owned the house," she said. "The police took our keys."

Eight days later they were driven out of Prnjavor. "We were beaten and pushed by the Serbs on the way to the buses," she said. "We wondered if we would make it over the river alive into Croatia."

Mirnes and his mother, like the others on the buses, prepared that night to sleep in a new, unfamiliar bed, still made up with the bedding used by the old owner and his wife. "All we have left from our old life together is each other, a few clothes, and Mirnes' stuffed bear," she said. "That bear has become the most precious thing we own."

Later that day, I wandered the streets of the town. The collective occupation of the houses was unsettling. On Ibre Hodzic Street one light shone from the rows of windows. I knocked on the door of the apartment and found three elderly women, two Serbs and a Muslim, intently listening to the news on a radio. The three friends were struggling, as they had for more than three years, to make sense of the latest diatribes unleashed by the Serbs or the Bosnian government, the political agreements that might augur peace, and the advances and defeats that marked the ebb and flow of war.

But in the end it had come down to this: The Bosnian government had just reclaimed this town from the Serbs, and nothing had changed except the victims. As a result of this reversal of fortunes, Dursuma Medić, a Muslim, would now have to watch over her two Serbian friends—who for the last three and a half years had taken care of her.

"We are three old women trying to survive a war," said Burka Bakovik, fifty-two, a Bosnian Serb. "We have been friends since childhood. None of this hatred ever touched us. We all protected Dursuma when the Serbs ruled. Now she protects us. The only news we wait for is peace, and that hasn't come yet."

As we spoke I could see Muslim soldiers busy painting over the slogans left by the Serbs on the walls outside. "Only one Bosnia, all the way to the Drina" and "Victory is our destiny," they wrote.

"The war began with words," said Seka Milanovik, sixty-eight, the other Bosnian Serb woman, "but none of us paid any attention. The extremist Serbs and Muslims were misfits, criminals and failures. But soon they held rallies and talked of racial purity, things like that. We dismissed them—until the violence began."

The women said the extremist groups soon partitioned the

city and surrounding villages into Serbian, Croatian, and Muslim areas. And each religious group turned to thugs for protection.

"I live in this apartment for two reasons," said Medić. "One is to protect my Serb friends. The other is because the Serbs burned my house down. I know what can happen when desperate people seek revenge. This is why I have to always be here."

"My daughter and two grandchildren fled with the crowds," said Bakovik. "I did not even have time to say goodbye. In a moment they were gone. Now I am alone and afraid. I do not want to be by myself in my apartment, so I stay here. We are all women; we all felt the same pangs in childbirth. We do not believe in war."

The loss of such social ties, the dependence on the state to dole out homes or property that was stolen, has an insidious effect on even the good and the just. Many must live with guilt and shame. They feel powerless. And those who have been abused and humiliated often search for those even weaker than they to vilify and blame for their predicament. In ethnic warfare this response feeds the racist cant of nationalist warlords who are with one hand thieving on unprecedented scales and with the other blaming the hapless minorities they are persecuting for the economic collapse and misery.

Displacement is one of the fundamental tools warlords and states use to prosecute a conflict. This is why ethnic leaders are so displeased when members of their minority group remain behind. The Croat and Serb and Muslim leaders in Bosnia often made secret deals to "trade" minorities, whether these families wanted to leave their homes or not. Such disruption helped fuel the conflict and sever communal ties with other groups.

"No one ever forgets a sudden depreciation of himself, for it is too painful," wrote the Bulgarian essayist Elias Canetti. "And the crowd as such never forgets its depreciation. The natural tendency afterwards is to find something which is worth even less than oneself, which one can despise as one was despised oneself. It is not enough to take over an old contempt and to maintain it at the same level. What is wanted is a dynamic process of humiliation. Something must be treated in such a way that it becomes worth less and less, as the unit of money did during the inflation. And this process must be continued until its object is reduced to a state of utter worthlessness. Then one can throw it away like paper, or repulp it."[18]

In the Bosnian town of Višegrad there is a graceful 400-year-old bridge, hewn of large off-white stones, that spans the emerald-green waters of the Drina River. The Nobel laureate Ivo Andrić centered his novel, *The Bridge on the Drina*, around the pumice structure, which he could see from his window as a boy. The book chronicles, over 350 years, the turbulent and often violent history of Višegrad and Bosnia. And as Andrić pointed out, the bridge has served as a kind of public theater in times of war and upheaval. Brigands and criminals were once impaled and executed on its stone flanks. "In all tales about personal, family or public events," Andrić wrote, "The words 'on the bridge' could always be heard."[19]

The steep wooded hillsides that plunge to the river have for centuries produced killers of appalling magnitude. During the Bosnian war the latest arose from Višegrad, Milan Lukić, along with his group of some fifteen well-armed companions. They too used the bridge as a prop to exterminate a Muslim community that had been there for centuries. Of the 14,500 Muslims who lived in Višegrad before the war, 3,000 are missing or dead.

The others are scattered around Bosnia, many living in poverty in overcrowded rooms and refugee centers.

In April 1992, when the conflict between the Bosnian Serbs and Muslims began, Milan Lukić returned from Serbia to his hometown. He gathered together a group of men, including his brother Miloš, his cousin Sredoje, and a waiter, Mitar Vasiljević. Lukić, who often went barefoot, called the group the Wolves. He set about robbing Muslim homes. The plunder quickly turned to killing. On May 18, Lukić burst into Dzemo Zukić's home and shot his wife, Bakha, in the back, according to neighbors who saw the shooting. He drove the terrified husband away in the family car, a red Volkswagen Passat. Zukić was never seen again. But the car became a harbinger of death.

The killings quickly became frenzied and common. On one occasion, Lukić used a rope to tie a man to his car and dragged him through the streets until he died. On at least two occasions, he herded large groups of Muslims into houses and set the buildings on fire. Zahra Turjacanin, her face and arms badly marred by the flames, escaped from one burning house on June 27 and raced screaming through the streets. Townspeople said she was the only survivor of seventy-one people inside. She now lives in France.

Lukić and his followers raped young girls held captive at the Vilina Vlas spa outside Višegrad. Jasna Ahmedspahić, a young woman, jumped to her death from a window of the spa after being raped for four days. Then Lukić began to drive his captives to the center of the bridge. Lukić and his men taunted their victims, who were made to stand on the walls of the bridge, before pushing them into the water and opening fire with automatic weapons. He stuffed pork in the mouths of his Muslim victims and began to beat them to death with metal rods. Bodies, bloated and discolored from beatings and knife slashes, floated down the river, getting caught in the undergrowth along the banks. In one village, Slap, twelve miles down river from Višegrad, the villagers said they buried 180 bodies that floated up on the banks. One man was found crucified on the back of a door. On another occasion they found a garbage bag filled with human heads.

Human beings become pawns, manipulated and moved around a board like chess pieces. Those struggling to survive in a morally bankrupt universe find that there are few restraints left. The perversion seeps into the behavior of those who came with noble sentiments to help. The U.N. peacekeeping troops in Bosnia, just as aid workers in Africa did, used the money and power they wielded to frequent or even run prostitution rings. The most notorious prostitution ring in Sarajevo during the war, one that catered to the peacekeepers, the foreign community, and the gangsters—all those with hard currency—was run by Ukrainian troops. They had also cornered the market on black market diesel, although they had the annoying habit of mixing it with water.

The reporters, diplomats, aid workers, and peacekeepers who travel into war zones, without the restraint of law and amid a sea of powerless people, often view themselves as entitled. They excuse immoral behavior because of the belief that the work they carry out is for a greater good—the rescue of those around them—which outweighs impropriety. They become giddy with the admiration and social status that come with being protected and privileged. Diplomats who entered Sarajevo restaurants would be applauded. They had servants, new jeeps, nice houses, and clout. And they had power unlike anything they experienced at home.

The conflict created a new elite, foreign class. It was a class that fed off of war's lawlessness and perversion. Students who spoke English in Bosnia and later Kosovo were soon making in a week more money than their teachers made in a year. Many lost all desire to study. It was not worth it. They paraded the new clothes and sunglasses they could buy with their dollars. Some began to look down on those around them with the same arrogance of those they worked for.

To those who are hungry, who spend all day in cold, gutted homes with no running water, who sleep on the concrete floors of overcrowded schools set up as refugee centers, who wake up and spend hours hunting for food or standing in long lines outside aid distribution centers, a little more humiliation is not much to endure. Many longed to enter the easy world of the elite. They would pay any price.

Many of those who set out to write their memoirs, or speak about the war, do so with shame. They know war's perversion. It corrupts nearly everyone. To be greeted by an indifferent public, by people who would rather not examine, in the end, their own darkness, makes the effort Herculean. After each war some struggle to tell us how the ego and vanity of commanders leads to the waste of lives and needless death, how they too became tainted, but the witnesses are soon ignored. It is not a pleasant message.

As would be the case with war literature in the millennia following its creation, *The Iliad* describes the bonds of honor between fellow warriors. Soldiers, while describing the closeness they feel in combat as friendship, are, as J. Glenn Gray wrote, probably deceived. The battlefield, with its ecstasy of destruction, its constant temptation of self-sacrifice, its evil bliss, is more about comradeship. The closeness of a unit, and even as a reporter one enters into that fraternity once you have been together under fire, is possible only with the wolf of death banging at the door. The feeling is genuine, but without the threat of violence and death it cannot be sustained.

There are few individual relationships—the only possible way to form friendships—in war. There are not the demands on us that there are in friendships. Veterans try to regain such feelings, but they fall short. Gray wrote that the "essential difference between comradeship and friendship consists, it seems to me, in a heightened awareness of the self in friendship and in the suppression of self-awareness in comradeship."[20]

Comrades seek to lose their identities in the relationship. Friends do not. "On the contrary," Gray wrote, "friends find themselves in each other and thereby gain greater self-knowledge and self-possession. They discover in their own breasts, as a consequence of their friendship, hitherto unknown potentialities for joy and understanding."[21]

The struggle to remain friends, the struggle to explore the often painful recesses of two hearts, to reach the deepest parts of another's being, to integrate our own emotions and desires with the needs of the friend, are challenged by the collective rush of war. There are fewer demands if we join the crowd and give our emotions over to the communal crusade.

The only solace comes from simple acts of kindness. They are the tiny, flickering candles in a cavern of darkness that sustain our common humanity.

There is a spiritual collapse after war. Societies struggle with the wanton destruction not only of property and cities but of those they loved. The erosion of morality and social responsibility becomes painfully evident in war's wake. Many feel used. By then it is too late. Those who drained the society flee, are killed, or live on in luxury from the profits of modern wars. Lethargy and passivity plague the populace that no longer has the energy or the moral fortitude to reconstitute society or fight back.

In the wake of war comes a normalization that levels victims and perpetrators. Victims and survivors are an awkward reminder of the collective complicity. Their presence inspires discomfort. So too with perpetrators, whose crimes were witnessed and even supported by many. But it is often the victims who suffer the worst bouts of guilt and remorse. They feel in debt to those who died. They know that it is not the best who survive war but often the selfish, the brutal, and the violent. Those who abandoned their humanity, betrayed their neighbors and friends, turned their back on their family, stole, cheated, killed, and stomped on the weak and infirm were often those who made it out alive. Many victims grasp, in a way the perpetrators do not, the inverted moral hierarchy. They see this inversion in their own struggle to survive. They realize, in a way that the perpetrators again do not, that the difference between the oppressed and the oppressors is not absolute. And they often wonder if they could have done more to save those who were lost around them.

"I might be alive in the place of another, at the expense of another; I might have usurped, that is, in fact killed," wrote Primo Levi, himself a survivor of the Holocaust.[22]

The physical marks of war are nearly erased from Sarajevo. Sheets of glass have been fitted into the high-rises, and the shell holes have been plastered over. The newly painted trolleys rumble nosily down the tracks of the central boulevard Zmaja od Bosne, known during the war as Snipers' Alley. Water, a commodity once so precious that mothers dashed under artillery fire to reach water trucks, gushes miraculously from the taps.

But the Bosnian capital, which once held together a blend of Muslims, Croats, and Serbs and hung on to life during almost four years of siege by the Bosnian Serbs, is a cultural wasteland. The city, once an artistic center, had a cosmopolitan feeling and a rich cultural and intellectual life. Marriages and friendships that crossed the ethnic divides were commonplace. Today, the ethnic mix and the liveliness it created are gone, along with hopes that the city would rekindle its old identity—hopes that have been disregarded by all three ethnic groups.

The $5.1 billion international reconstruction effort, which has physically mended Sarajevo, masks despair. The smooth, plaster facades of apartment blocks, painted purple, red, blue, and yellow, shelter people who for the most part survive on the beneficence of others.

Beneath the physical rehabilitation, however, there is another reality. Men, out of work, often wounded physically or emotionally, waste hours in dingy coffee shops. Many of the young gather in the lines for visas outside foreign embassies. At night they meet in jammed, smoky clubs like Fis or The Stage where they can buy marijuana, Ecstasy, and heroin. An army of war invalids lies trapped indoors. Most of them lack proper medical attention, and many spend their days alone in rooms, tended by elderly parents.

"My son is inside," said an angry seventy-year-old man, who would not give his name, as he stood outside his small house fitting new aluminum drainpipes to the roof. "He can't get up. Every night my wife has to go in and turn him over so he can go to the bathroom."

Thousands in the city, where half of the work force is jobless, live in apartments that belong to someone else, someone who lives across the ethnic gulf, still a universe away in this partitioned country.

Muslims now account for more than 90 percent of the population in this city of 350,000 and with the widespread uprooting of people during and after the war, only 20 percent of the city's residents are natives of the city. The siege and the drastic changes that followed it have left behind exhaustion and bewilderment that makes routine life daunting.

"I will never again be able to live such a strong, horrible, and wonderful life," said Boba Lizdek, thirty-two, a book translator. Lizdek, a Serb who stayed in Sarajevo through the war, said that since then she had lost her focus and purpose. "It is as if I see life through pieces of a mirror that lies in fragments," she said.

The suburb of Dobrinja, built as the athletes' village for the 1984 Winter Olympics, was on the front line during the war. Sections of the town are in ruins, the walls and roofs gone, the bricks and cement chewed up by shell and bullet holes. Crude grave markers poke up at odd angles from tiny, overgrown parks and lonely patches of ground.

The renovated buildings, often next to the ruins, gleam with spotless white plaster and terra-cotta tiled roofs. The balconies hold boxes of carnations. The streets are quiet.

Murdija Badzić, fifty-one, lived in a small apartment that she and her husband rebuilt for $10,000. It was clean, with new carpets, a semicircular blue sofa in the living room, and freshly painted walls.

In June 1992, Serbian troops occupied the Dobrinja area. Badzić was herded barefoot along with her children to a prison camp, where they were held for two weeks.

The family stayed away for four years out of fear, she said, and when she returned in 1996, all the mementos of her life, her photos, the children's favorite toys, the wedding gifts, and the collection of trinkets that remind couples of the passage of time together, had vanished.

The two-room apartment held nothing of the old life. The only photo on the wall was of her eldest son, Husein, a soldier killed in the war. She and her husband lived with their remaining two sons. The young men, unemployed since the end of the war, had applied to emigrate to the United States. When Badzić spoke of the war, her youngest son, Aladin, twenty-four, abruptly left the room.

"Forgive him," she said. "He cannot talk about the war. He cannot hear about it."

During the family's detention, Aladin, who was sixteen at the time, was severely beaten by Serbian soldiers and threatened with mock executions. He did not speak for two months after he was released.

In the empty street below, Huso Kovač, fifty-eight, swung himself forward with the help of hand-held aluminum crutches. He said he disliked spending days in his apartment, which previously belonged to a Serb. He moved laboriously about the neighborhood, resting at times on the cement walls and staring at the road.

Before the war Kovač worked in Sutjeska, the national park that was the site of a major Partisan battle against the Nazis in World War II. When he spoke of the yearly anniversaries, which always saw the arrival of Tito, the dictator, his eyes lit up. It was the only time he smiled.

He lost his leg in 1993 as he and his Muslim neighbors fled under mortar fire from Sutjeska over Mount Igman to Sarajevo. His only son died in the war. His daughter's husband was also killed. She cared for their two small children alone on her widow's pension.

"I don't trust anyone anymore," he said. "This is what the war has taught me, not to trust."

He shifted his hands to grip the handles of the crutches and moved away.

5

THE HIJACKING AND RECOVERY OF MEMORY

Our people's lives pass, bitter and empty, among
malicious, vengeful thoughts and periodic revolts.
To anything else, they are insensitive and inacces-
sible. One sometimes wonders whether the spirit of
the majority of the Balkan peoples has not been
forever poisoned and that, perhaps, they will never
again be able to do anything other then suffer violence, or inflict it.

•

IVO ANDRIĆ
Conversation with Goya: Signs, Bridges

HAGOB H. ASADOURIAN, LIKE MANY SURVIVORS OF
genocide, communes with shadows. Some are dark and
frightening, like the shades of Turkish soldiers, who in 1915
herded him and his family from his Armenian village, leaving
him to watch his mother and four of his sisters die of typhus in
the Syrian desert. Some are sweet, revolving around the raucous

Armenian-language plays performed in the 1920s at the Yiddish Theater at Madison Avenue and Twenty-seventh Street in Manhattan. And some are poignant, like the reunion with his sole surviving sister, thirty-nine years after they lost each other one night near the Dead Sea as they fled with a ragged band of Armenian orphans from Syria to Jerusalem.

But his battle to preserve memory, the theme of his fourteen books, did not save him or his generation from the destructive march of time. And time, to the rapidly vanishing community of exiled Armenians, will soon finish the work that, he says, was begun by the Turkish army more than eighty-five years ago.

The Turks have spent most of the past century denying, with rather startling success, the Armenian genocide of 1915, when the Ottoman Empire, fearing a nationalist revolt, forced two million Armenians into the Syrian desert to die. The few surviving Armenians no longer ask to go home. They do not ask for restitution. They ask simply to have the memory of their obliteration acknowledged. It is a moral obsession, the lonely legacy passed onto the third and fourth generation who no longer speak Armenian but who carry within them the seeds of resentment that will not be quashed.

Asadourian's latest book, *The Smoldering Generation*, was, he said, "about the inevitable loss of our culture."

"No one takes the place of those who are gone," the ninety-seven-year-old writer said when I visited him at his home in Tenafly, New Jersey. He was seated in front of a picture window that looked out on a carefully groomed garden. "Your children do not understand you in this country. You cannot blame them."

As he spoke, his middle-aged son, John, who has used a wheelchair since a stroke, jerked himself into position behind his father. He listened, his head cocked slightly to one side, with a grimace.

Although there were once ten major Armenian-language daily newspapers in the United States, there is just one left, published in California. Armenian clubs have closed, social societies have been disbanded, and cultural events have dwindled. Proceedings of Armenian meetings, when they take place, are usually in English (except at church affairs, where Armenian clergy nearly always speak in Armenian first, then English). Asadourian said that he had accepted that his writing would not halt the slide to obliteration of the language. (His two sons were raised speaking Armenian; his granddaughter speaks it, but does not write it very well.)

Rather, he writes to give a voice to the 331 people with whom he trudged into Syria in September 1915. Only twenty-nine of those people survived.

"You can never really write what happened anyway," Asadourian said. "It is too ghoulish. I still fight with myself to remember it as it was. You write because you have to. It all wells up inside of you. It is like a hole that fills constantly with water and no amount of bailing will empty it. This is why I continue."

His passion, however, burns deep. He refused to halt the painful story of his deportation despite having to reach for a bottle of pills. He took a deep breath before plunging into the last bit of detail, one he had left out of the lengthy chronology.

"When it came time to bury my mother, I had to get two other small boys to help me carry her body up to a well where they were dumping the corpses," he said. "We did this so the jackals would not eat them. The stench was terrible. There were swarms of black flies buzzing over the opening. We pushed her in feet first, and the other boys, to escape the smell, ran down the hill. I stayed. I had to watch. I saw her head, as she fell, bang on one side of the well and then the other before she disappeared. At the time, I did not feel anything at all."

He stopped, visibly shaken.

"What kind of a son is that?" he asked hoarsely.

I had seen and felt it before, the awful indifference to pain, even your own. But just because he did not feel anything at the moment he released his mother's body did not mean he did not care. He had spent his whole life honoring the memory of his mother. He had suffered, in later years, that moment of her hasty burial with an awful intensity. It was a display of the curious guilt of the victims who often carry with them torments not borne by the perpetrators of the crimes.

The house fell silent. Asadourian's son, as motionless as his father during the story, flipped the electric switch on his chair and rolled out of the room.

The Turkish government still vigorously denies the event. It says that some of the Armenians killed were rebels during World War I and others were victims of the fighting and the widespread famine. The Turks claim they escorted Armenians away from the fighting for their own safety. They concede only that, because of the war, some unfortunate incidents took place.

Much of the world of the Armenians, a people first mentioned by the ancient Greeks and Persians in the 6th century B.C., has been reduced to dusty, forgotten relics in present-day Turkey. After World War I, about 25,000 Armenians came to the United States. Some of their tales survive in small American collections of Armenian literature and poetry, like the 15,000 volumes in the Zohrab Center in New York. These books lie unread by all but a few scholars. Little of the work has been translated.

The murder of more than one million Armenians in Turkey is often cited as the opening act for the genocidal campaigns that convulsed the twentieth century. Although the Allied powers condemned the Turks during World War I, there was no effort to hold them accountable for actions against the Armenians. The magnitude of the deaths and ultimate indifference may have led Hitler, on the eve of the invasion of Poland, to remind his followers, "Who still speaks of the extermination of the Armenians?"

The globe is dotted with such anonymous burial pits. They are physical reminders of justice denied. Yet they have a startling power to plague the murderers decades after the event. These atrocities—denied by the perpetrators and sanctified by the victims—leave huge chasms between peoples. They serve to create two distinct and antagonistic histories. It is only with an historical consensus that there can be reconciliation.

The return of historical memory restores a common language to the one usurped by war. The 1991 exhumations in the Katyn Forest outside Kalinin for the thousands of Polish officers executed by the Soviets in World War II permitted an historical narrative that could be accepted by the Russians and the Poles. What followed, once the truth was exposed, was the collapse of the Soviet Union. The exhumations in Cambodia, El Salvador, and the Bosnian town of Srebrenica are part of the same process. It is these exhumations, these final acknowledgments, that bring down regimes and force the restoration of history. But until such a moment happens, the wartime regimes zealously guard the lie.

During conflicts, these hidden burial places are spoken of in hushed and nervous whispers. As wars wind to a close the killers make frantic and often futile efforts to hide their crimes. They bulldoze fields where bodies are buried, as they did in Srebrenica, dynamite mine shafts where bodies were dumped, or dissolve the corpses in acid. But the industrial-scale killing of the twentieth century makes such erasure difficult. And years later there often is a dogged and methodical effort, usually by lonely dissidents, to uncover the past. These statisticians wield with index cards the fate of despots, the return of historical memory and, finally, hope.

I was taken to a school in northern Iraq days after Iraqi soldiers withdrew from the region following the Gulf War. Kurdish rebels there told me that under the concrete in the schoolyard were hundreds of bodies. They vowed to smash through the concrete and dig them up.

When I moved across central Bosnia with advancing Muslim troops after the NATO bombing campaign of 1995, survivors would enter villages even while the fighting was still dying down and point out burial sites. These sites, one sensed, were as important as their houses and personal property. Muslim officials who traveled with the army carried long handwritten lists of names of missing from the war. They began, even amid the skirmishes, to hunt for the graves that held the bodies of hundreds, perhaps thousands, of victims massacred when the Serbs swept through this area to drive out the Muslims years earlier. I drove with them to several sites. I watched as they marked them off with rope for excavation. Near a hamlet called Pudin Han, we found a cave that had human bones poking up out of a large circular depression. Another site, known as Crvena Zemlja, or "red earth," had already given up bones and clothing. In Prhovo, a vacant ruin perched on a hillside about five miles north of Ključ, a man who witnessed a mass killing led these authorities to a spot where he told us dozens of victims of the massacre lay buried.

Senad Medanović, twenty-five, a factory worker turned soldier, returned to his home with us after three years. He climbed the steep dirt track leading to his village, in the company of three other Muslims. All were armed with AK–47 assault rifles. The men scanned the dense undergrowth for the pockets of Bosnian Serb soldiers who were still hiding in the rolling, pine-forested hills.

Medanović, ignoring the periodic crackle of small-arms fire, headed for the spot, a rough plot of land across from the gutted remains of his two-story house. He stood there and told me about the day the Serbs came. It was on the morning of June 1, 1992. He saw several hundred Bosnian Serb militiamen and Yugoslav Army troops surround the village of about two dozen houses. They herded the families into the center of the village and opened fire with automatic weapons and heavy machine guns. Mingled with the group were Muslim families from some neighboring villages.

"I was over here," said he, standing near the edge of a field. "I did not trust the Serbs, and I stood as far away as I could. I told my family they would kill us, but they did not believe such a thing was possible. When they started to shoot I ran. I could hear the screams of the women and the children. I could hear the awful noise of the guns. I ran across the field into the woods. The Serbs around the village fired at me, but I was able to reach the woods and hide in the undergrowth."

The Serbs spent the night drinking and looting the houses in the village, he said, and the next morning he watched as they searched the woods for any survivors. They rounded up about forty men, stripped them, and marched them down the road with their hands tied.

"I saw them shoot two at the edge of the village," he said. "When I was captured six days later, on the run, and taken to the Manjaca concentration camp, I found nine of the forty who had survived, including one of my brothers. The others had been murdered. The survivors told me where the mass grave was. They told me my mother, and the rest of my family, were dead. We ten are all that remain from Prhovo."

Lanky and bearded, he climbed through the window of his former house and began to search among the blackened debris. He pulled out the tattered remains of a blue shirt and hugged it.

"This belonged to one of my nephews," he said, "one of the twins."

The bloody campaign by the Bosnian Serbs to rid this part of Bosnia of Muslims, who had lived here for more than 500 years, left survivors vowing to take revenge. Medanović said he would hunt down the two Serbian commanders whom he said led the massacre.

"The two beasts who directed this slaughter were Marko Adamović and Ratko Buvac," he said. "We all knew the Serbian nationalists from Ključ before they came to kill us. We heard them preach hatred against the Muslims. And we saw them as they entered the village that morning to direct the killings."

But tempering his hatred was his relief at the chance to at least honor the memories of the family he lost, his mother, five of his six brothers, his only sister, his uncle, and two nephews.

He stood over the field that held the bodies.

"Here is where my family and my village lie now," he said. "And God has permitted me to survive to come back and give them a decent burial."

It was dusk and we were a small group, lightly armed, on a hill that still had bands of fleeing Serb soldiers. We started down the dirt track. But when Medanović saw the shattered black granite tombs of his father and grandfather, who died before

the war, he knelt. He tried to arrange the pieces of the head-
stones to spell out their names once again.

"Can you read their names now?" he asked me. "Can you see
who was buried here?"

Wartime leaders, who know that exposing the murders
means the loss of their own legitimacy and discrediting of the
myth, harass and denounce the Cassandras who cry out for justice and historical accountability. The effort to give a name to
the victims and killers begins a collective act of repentance, a
national catharsis. The process, as seen in South Africa's Truth
and Reconciliation Commission, is the only escape. And while
justice is not always done—in South Africa the full admission of
crimes saw killers granted an amnesty—dignity, identity, and
most important, memory are returned. This, for many families,
is enough.

Only rarely do some of the top leaders end up in jail. Usually
those who pay the price—if there is one to be paid—are the
lowly gunmen who are tried and imprisoned to take the heat off
of their commanders. Most of those who carry out war crimes,
however, are never punished. They are allowed to fade away in
retirement, whispered about but never finally condemned. There
are powerful institutions, security services, armed forces, and
ministries of the interior, that may permit some facts to be
exposed but will rarely permit a society to ascribe any responsibility to the actual state organs that directed the killings. Yet
despite the inevitable injustice of any investigation, the power
it has to restore memory is vital for recovery from war.

"The struggle of man against power," wrote the novelist
Milan Kundera, "is the struggle of memory against forgetting."[1]

I walked one afternoon over the cavernous pits and gorges
scattered throughout the hills above the Italian port city of Trieste. These hold dark secrets from the twilight days of World

War II, secrets that still disturb Italy and its Balkan neighbors. The pits, covered with tons of debris, are believed to contain hundreds, perhaps thousands, of corpses. The bodies are those of Italians and Yugoslavs who opposed the Yugoslav Communist takeover of the city in May 1945, along with scores of captured German soldiers. But attempts to investigate, even after five decades, have gone nowhere.

Trieste is a port city that for most of the twentieth century sat on the edge of the volcanic upheavals that tore apart the European monarchies and made up the front lines of the Cold War. It changed hands a half dozen times. James Joyce and Rainer Maria Rilke lived here. The notorious commander in the Spanish civil war, Commandante Carlos, came from Trieste, as did the writer Italo Svevo. The city, seedy, neglected, is no longer of any geopolitical significance. But the scars of its past infect the air. Old men with sad stories gather every afternoon in the seaside coffee shops.

In May 1945, Tito's Communist Partisans in Yugoslavia, after a bitter guerrilla war against the German and Croatian fascists, pursued the retreating forces toward Italy. The Partisan army seized the Istrian Peninsula, in the northern Adriatic, and raced on toward Trieste. The Partisans' forty-day occupation of Trieste and their hunt for German soldiers, Italian and Croatian fascists, and suspected opponents of Communism nearly led to a clash with Allied forces. In June, the Yugoslavs withdrew to the hinterlands, but Trieste was not handed back to Italy until 1954. Today the city has 230,000 people, many of them from Italian families who were forced out of Yugoslavia after the war.

Trieste in May 1945 was a chaotic city filled with cornered German, Croatian, and Italian soldiers who continued to fight despite Italy's capitulation in 1943. Scores of accused fascists were paraded daily by the Partisans through the cobblestone

streets to Yugoslav military courts. Most were quickly condemned to death and shot, or thrown alive into gorges and pits
around the city.

Many Slovenes in Trieste at the time, ecstatic at the downfall
of Italian fascism, greeted the Partisans as liberators and
assisted in manhunts by the Yugoslav secret police. During the
occupation, at least 3,500 residents of Trieste, along with an
unknown number of Yugoslavs, Italians, and Germans who
were trapped in the city, were shot and thrown into the fissures,
or *foibe*, of the Carso mountain range, the eastern end of the
Italian Alps. Thousands more were deported, and many perished in Yugoslav detention camps.

A secret British-American intelligence report of September
1945, made public just a few years ago, is filled with accounts by
witnesses to partisan atrocities. A Roman Catholic priest, Don
Sceck, told the investigators that on May 2, 1945, a group of 150
fascists were swiftly sentenced and then mowed down by partisan troops with machine guns in Basovizza, a small Slovene-
speaking village just outside Trieste. The corpses, he said, were
thrown into the huge Basovizza caverns, now a memorial to the
victims. The next day he saw a group of about 250 prisoners at
the mouth of the Basovizza pit.

"These persons were questioned and tried in the presence of
all the populace, who accused them," the priest said in the
report. "As soon as one of them was questioned, four or five
women rushed up to them and accused them of having murdered or tortured one of their relatives, or of having burned
down their homes. The accused persons were butted and
struck, and always admitted the crimes ascribed to them."

In war, death is often anonymous. When it is impossible to
find out whether someone is dead or alive there is no closure,
no way to fix the end of a life with a time and a place. The

atrocity is compounded by the atrocity committed against memory. The lack of closure tortures and deforms those who wait for an answer. This sacrilege against memory gnaws at survivors. Regimes use murder and anonymous death to keep their citizens off balance, agitated, and disturbed. It fuels war's collective insanity. But it must be rectified if healing is to take place.

The misery often spawns predators. Families in Iraq pay huge bribes to find out whether relatives are dead or alive. Occultists promise to put people in touch with those who are missing, often stringing families along for weeks as they pass on supposed messages from prisons, mines, or work camps. I have sat in on such encounters in El Salvador and Algeria, watching as tearful women struggle to believe that they are communicating with missing sons or husbands. These women, repeatedly rebuffed by the security forces and government bureaucrats, find comfort in mediums, although most realize after a few months that they have been had. Memory, even manufactured memory, seems better for a while than silence. Hope, however farfetched, is prolonged. But the ache over the missing eventually evolves into a single need—the recovery of the body.

A film by the French director Bertrand Tavernier, *Life and Nothing But* (1989), captured this need, with two women combing the remains of an old battlefield, looking for the same corpse. The Chilean writer Ariel Dorfman touched on the same theme in his novel *Widows*. He wrote of a village in Greece during World War II where a body is discovered washed up on a riverbank. It is battered beyond recognition. An elderly peasant woman, who has lost her two sons, her husband, and her father, claims the body and refuses to give it to the authorities. Soon thirty-seven women who have lost relatives also claim the body, setting off a struggle over the corpse and the military dictatorship that thought it could erase history.[2]

The violence of war is random. It does not make sense. And many of those who struggle with loss also struggle with the knowledge that the loss was futile and unnecessary. This leaves psychological wounds among survivors as well as veterans. Many of the soldiers who fought in Vietnam must grapple with the realization that there was no higher purpose to the war, that the sacrifice was a waste. It is easier to believe the myth that makes such loss noble and necessary, despite the glaring contradictions.

In Argentina in the 1970s and 1980s most of the 20,000 "disappeared" in the Dirty War were not armed radicals but labor leaders, community organizers, leftist intellectuals, and student organizers. Few of them had any connection to guerrilla campaigns. Indeed, by the time of the 1976 Argentine coup the armed guerrilla movements, such as the Montoneros, had largely been wiped out. They had never been a threat to the state, but the abductions spawned a vast underground prison system that soon existed mostly to extort money from the victims' families.

In Marguerite Feitlowitz's *The Lexicon of Terror*, she writes of the experiences of one Argentine prisoner, a physicist named Mario Villani.[3] The collapse of the moral universe of the torturers is displayed when, in between torture sessions, the guards take Villani and a few pregnant women prisoners to an amusement park. They make them ride the kiddie train. A guard, whose nom de guerre is Blood, brings his six- or seven-year-old daughter into the camp to meet Villani. Villani runs into one of his principal torturers a few years later, a man known in the camps as Julian the Turk. Julian recommends that Villani go see another of his former prisoners to ask for a job.

Julian the Turk was free because military pressure put a stop to the post-junta trials. After the convictions of five of the nine commanders, repeated military uprisings persuaded President Raúl Alfonsin to propose laws setting a time limit on prosecutions and exempting all men below a certain rank from any prosecution. The Argentine congress quickly passed both laws. Alfonsin's successor, Carlos Saúl Menem, then pardoned the commanders who had been convicted, along with several dozen other prisoners. In neighboring Chile, General Augusto Pinochet sits protected in his lifetime Senate seat, immune from prosecution.

Until the lie is discredited and history is recovered, societies continue to speak in euphemisms. They use words to mask reality. It was the Argentine junta that gave us words like *desaparecido* (disappeared person, almost always a euphemism for someone who had been secretly executed), *chupado* (sucked up, or kidnapped) and *trasladar* (transfer, a euphemism for take away to be killed). Terms like these blunt the campaign of terror. On the battlefield it is much the same. Soldiers get "waxed" rather than killed. Victims who are burned to death are "toasted."

The Soviet writer Vasily Grossman's novel *Life and Fate* was about the fight to remember and defeat anonymous death. The mother in the novel, based on Grossman's own mother, was massacred along with 30,000 other people, most of them Jews, by the Nazis in his native town of Berdichev in Ukraine during World War II. In one chapter he wrote the letter he believed his mother would have written to him before she was executed, a final message to her only child. The letter revealed the gaping wound that Grossman, who was unable to communicate with his mother before her execution, must have endured.

Describing neighbors who, given license by the Nazi occupiers, have turned her into a pariah, the mother wrote dispas-

sionately. "I really don't know which is worse," she said, "gloat-
ing spite, or these pitying glances like people cast at a mangy,
half-dead cat."

Then she wrote: "But now I've seen that the people who
shout most loudly about delivering Russia from the Jews are the
very ones who cringe like lackeys before the Germans, ready to
betray their country for 30 pieces of German silver. And
strange people from the outskirts of town seize our rooms, our
blankets, our clothes. It must have been people like them who
killed doctors at the time of the cholera riots. And then there
are people whose souls have just withered, people who are
ready to go along with anything evil—anything so as not to be
suspected of disagreeing with whoever's in power."[4]

When *Life and Fate* was completed in 1960, four years before
Grossman died, the K.G.B. seized the manuscript. He was
never allowed to publish again.

It is rare that we are able to expose the crimes of a regime
while it is still in power. This is usually part of the long recovery
process once the killers have been ousted. But in Iraq we had
the unique opportunity to peer inside the guts of Saddam Hussein's regime and confront a regime with its crimes.

After the Gulf War, the Kurds in northern Iraq were given
a safe area that was under the protection of NATO warplanes.
With the Iraqi military gone from the area, it became possible to
investigate the crimes of Saddam Hussein's regime even as he
remained in power. Mass graves, torture chambers, elaborate
prison systems, and secret police files attested to the inner workings of one of the region's harshest dictatorships. Gravesites
regularly contained hundreds of bodies of men, women, and
children. I stood one afternoon as diggers uncovered the
remains of 1,500 soldiers who had apparently been executed

after refusing to fight in the war during the 1980s against Iran. Until the bodies were identified, the dead had "disappeared."

Kurdish leaders estimated that more than 180,000 Kurds had vanished at the hands of the Iraqi secret police. The Iraqis killed anyone, including young children, whom they believed supported the outlawed Kurdish guerrilla movement or belonged to a family that had ties with the Kurdish rebels. More than 4,000 villages—primarily those near the Turkish or Iranian borders that were regarded by the Iraqis as sanctuaries for Kurdish rebels—were demolished under the program, which reached its peak of intensity in 1987 and 1988, toward the end of the Iran-Iraq war.

The killing sites are often found a few feet from the mass graves. On Kalowa Hill, five tires filled with cement were all that remained of the spot where many people were shot to death. Earthen embankments bordered the site. Prisoners, blindfolded with their hands tied behind ten-foot metal poles, had their feet planted in the cement and were shot.

Of course those who lived nearby knew that something was happening. When I spoke with those in the vicinity of Kalowa Hill, they said they often heard screams and volleys of shots, but were threatened if they tried to peer into the high-walled compound. Stray dogs used to trot back with human bones or a fleshy limb, after getting inside the compound. The Iraqi guards began to shoot the dogs.

At Kalowa Hill I stood with my seven bodyguards. The Iraqi regime had put a price on the heads of all foreigners who worked in the Kurdish-controlled areas. Several had been shot and killed, including a German photographer I worked with. We watched a Kurdish woman, Pershan Hassan, clamber quickly up the dirt track leading to the site. As she hurried for-

ward, she clutched to her chest a framed black and white pho-
tograph of a young boy. At the top of the rise, a crowd that had
gathered parted silently as she stumbled forward.

She suddenly stopped and let out a gasp of pain and recognition. Before her, nine years after he had disappeared from a
schoolyard, lay the skeletal remains of her thirteen-year-old son,
Shafiq. A faded blue blindfold was tightly wrapped around his
skull and spent bullets were scattered among his now dark-
brown bones.

"I know him by his clothes," she whispered, her voice breaking as she lifted the garments and kissed them. "I raised him
without a father."

In all such scenes there is grief. But there is also a palpable
sense of relief. The lost son or husband is recovered. The salutary effect makes it possible to go forward in life. It took the
efforts of Iraq's leading dissident, Kanan Mikaya and Human
Rights Watch, to make sure that truckloads of documents,
including photographs and videotapes of executions, were
transported out of northern Iraq to safety.

I leafed through the long, typewritten lists that were in abandoned secret police headquarters that chronicled killing after
killing, sometimes for what seemed to be trivial offenses. One
man was sentenced to death because he had a picture of a rebel
Kurdish leader in his wallet.

A picture I found in a police file showed what appeared to
be three Iraqi officials squatting like big game hunters next to
the slumped body of a man who was recently killed. One of the
Iraqis, wearing a beret, grinned while holding a knife to the
corpse's neck. It was, once again, the strange need by killers to
display human corpses as trophies.

I watched hours of videotapes shot by the Iraqi secret police of their own executions. Prisoners would be tied to poles, riddled with gunfire, and left slumped on the ground. There was a deadening sameness to it all and a strange and sickening fascination. The recording of such acts came out of a collapse of the moral universe, a world where right and wrong had been turned upside down. In the world of war, perversion may become moral; guilt may be honor, and the gunning down of unarmed people, including children, may be defined as heroic. In this world the "liquidation" of the enemy, with the enemy defined as simply the other, is part of the redemption of the nation.

The hill in northern Iraq began to draw hundreds of Kurdish women looking for lost children or husbands. The plaintive cries of those who recovered the remains of their loved ones would rise above the murmur of the crowd. Most, however, watched mutely day after day.

And circling the huge pit, a pit hacked at by men with shovels and pickaxes, were the gaunt survivors of the vast secret police prison network. They spoke of torture, beatings, hunger, and the long severance, sometimes for years, of all contact with the outside world.

A few weeks later, I traveled to Shorish, a suburb of Sulaimaniya, with Jamal Aziz Amin, a courtly forty-five-year-old headmaster. We entered a soundproofed room in the darkened remains of the Sulaimaniya central security prison, where he spent a year in detention. Large hooks hung from the ceiling where Amin, an Iraqi Kurd, was suspended during torture. He was handcuffed behind his back, he said, and hoisted onto the hooks at the wrist. He said he was stripped, questioned about his ties to Kurdish guerrilla groups, and given electric shocks until he fell unconscious.

"You would scream," he told me, "and it would sound as if you were yelling from the bottom of a deep, deep well."

The huge prison, its tiers of cells piled one on top of the other, stood bleak and deserted. When it was attacked in 1991 by Kurdish fighters and enraged civilians, 300 Iraqi secret policemen and guards, including the warden, held out for three days. None of the defenders survived.

Amin and his fellow Kurdish prisoners, after the attack, had the rare experience of standing over the bodies of many of their torturers.

"We wanted them to all come back to life," he said, "so we could kill them again."

At the prison, inmates subsisted on thin soup, bread, and weak tea. Amin said that by the time he was released, he had lost sixty pounds. The walls of the cells, many marked with crudely drawn calendars, carried the messages of those who tried to leave some testament, some record of their suffering.

"These were my friends, arrested with me," a prisoner named Ahmed Mohammed wrote, listing five names. "All were executed."

Another prisoner had written a message to his mother: "Oh, mother, in this dark room my dreams trouble me and I shake. Then comes the kicking against my door and a voice telling me to get up. It is time for my interrogation. I awake to the unconscious." Amin wound his way to the crude latrine, a hole in the cement, at the end of a corridor of cells.

"I wanted to show you this," he said, a small shaft of light streaming in from a tiny, barred window fourteen feet above him. "Here is where we would come at night so we could pull ourselves up the walls to hear the sound of the dogs barking in the distance. To hear the dogs, this was everything for us."

Historical memory is hijacked by those who carry out war. They seek, when the memory challenges the myth, to obliterate or hide the evidence that exposes the myth as lie. The destruction is pervasive, aided by an establishment, including the media, which apes the slogans and euphemisms parroted by the powerful. Because nearly everyone in wartime is complicit, it is difficult for societies to confront their own culpability and the lie that led to it.

But societies that do not confront the past remain trapped in an Oz-like world, a world whose most important truths are felt—then repressed—every day, a world where official lies are perpetuated by a vast bureaucracy. For the rift between Trieste's Slovene and Italian communities to be healed, the graves outside the city will have to be exhumed. The commissions set up in Chile, Argentina, and Brazil, as well as the international war crimes tribunal in The Hague, were created to give these nations a common vocabulary. Until then the factions will not communicate.

There probably can never be full recovery of memory, but in order to escape the miasma of war there must be some partial rehabilitation, some recognition of the denial and perversion, some new way given to speak that lays bare the myth as fantasy and the cause as bankrupt. The whole truth may finally be too hard to utter, but the process of healing only begins when we are able to at least acknowledge the tragedy and accept our share of the blame.

6

THE CAUSE

... all my means are sane, my motive and my object mad.

•

CAPTAIN AHAB IN *Moby Dick*

WHEN I STEPPED OFF AN ARMY C-130 MILITARY transport in Dhahran, Saudi Arabia, to cover the Persian Gulf War, I was escorted to a room with several dozen other reporters and photographers. I was told to sign a paper that said I would abide by the severe restrictions placed on the press by the U.S. military. The restrictions authorized "pool reporters" to be escorted by the military on field trips. The rest of the press would sit in hotel rooms and rewrite the bland copy filed by the pool or use the pool video and photos. This was an agreement I violated the next morning, when I went into the field without authorization. The rest of the war, during which I spent more than half my time dodging military police and trying to talk my way into units, was a forlorn and lonely struggle against the heavy press control.

The Gulf War made war fashionable again. It was a cause the nation willingly embraced. It gave us media-manufactured

heroes and a heady pride in our military superiority and technology. It made war fun. And the blame, as in many conflicts,
lay not with the military but the press. Television reporters hap-
pily disseminated the spoon-fed images that served the propaganda effort of the military and the state. These images did little
to convey the reality of war. Pool reporters, those guided
around in groups by the military, wrote about "our boys" eating
packaged army food, practicing for chemical weapons attacks,
and bathing out of buckets in the desert. It was war as spectacle,
war as entertainment. The images and stories were designed to
make us feel good about our nation, about ourselves. The Iraqi
families and soldiers being blown to bits by huge iron fragmentation bombs just over the border in Iraq were faceless and
nameless phantoms.

The notion that the press was used in the war is incorrect.
The press wanted to be used. It saw itself as part of the war
effort. Most reporters sent to cover a war don't really want to go
near the fighting. They do not tell this to their editors and
indeed will moan and complain about restrictions. The handful
who actually head out into the field have a bitter enmity with the
hotel-room warriors. But even those who do go out are guilty of
distortion. For we not only believe the myth of war and feed
recklessly off of the drug but also embrace the cause. We may
do it with more skepticism. We certainly expose more lies and
misconceptions. But we believe. We all believe. When you stop
believing you stop going to war.

The record of the press as mythmaker stretches at least from
William Howard Russell's romantic account of the 1854 charge
of the Light Brigade—he called the event "the pride and splen-
dour of war"—to Afghanistan after September 11, 2001. The
true victims of war, because we rarely see or hear them (as is

usual in most war reporting), faintly exist. I boycotted the pool system, but my reports did not puncture the myth or question the grand crusade to free Kuwait. I allowed soldiers to grumble. I shed a little light on the lies spread to make the war look like a coalition, but I did not challenge in any real way the patriotism and jingoism that enthused the crowds back home. We all used the same phrases. We all looked at Iraq through the same lens. And at night, when the huge bombers dropped tons of high explosives on Iraqi positions, lighting up the night sky with red fireballs, I felt immeasurable reassurance along with the soldiers.

It has been rare in every war I have covered to find a reporter who did not take sides. I believed—and still do—that in Bosnia and El Salvador, there were victims and oppressors in the conflict. But along with this acknowledgment comes for many a disturbing need to portray the side they back in their own self-image. The leftist Sandinistas in Nicaragua, the rebels in El Salvador and Guatemala, the African National Congress, the Muslim-led government in Sarajevo, or the opposition in Serbia were all endowed with the qualities they did not possess. The Christian ethicist Reinhold Niebuhr warned us that moral choice is not between the moral and the immoral, but between the immoral and the less immoral.

War finds its meaning in death. The cause is built on the backs of victims, portrayed always as innocent. Indeed, most conflicts are ignited with martyrs, whether real or created. The death of an innocent, one who is perceived as emblematic of the nation or the group under attack, becomes the initial rallying point for war. These dead become the standard-bearers of the cause and all causes feed off a steady supply of corpses.

Following the Iraqi invasion of Kuwait, it was widely disseminated that Iraqi soldiers removed hundreds of Kuwaiti babies from incubators and left them to die on hospital floors. The story, when we arrived in Kuwait and were able to check with doctors at the hospitals, turned out to be false. But by then the tale had served its purpose. The story came from a fifteen-year-old Kuwaiti who identified herself only as "Nayirah" when she tearfully testified before the Congressional Human Rights Caucus on October 10, 1990. She said she had watched fifteen infants being taken from incubators in the Al-Adan Hospital in Kuwait City by Iraqi soldiers who "left the babies on the cold floor to die." Nayirah turned out later to be the daughter of the Kuwaiti ambassador to the United States, Saud Nasir al-Sabah. She did not grant interviews after the war and it was never established whether she was actually in the country when the invasion took place.

Elias Canetti wrote, "It is the first death which infects everyone with the feeling of being threatened. It is impossible to overrate the part played by the first dead man in the kindling of wars. Rulers who want to unleash war know very well that they must procure or invent a first victim. It need not be anyone of particular importance, and can even be someone quite unknown. Nothing matters except his death; and it must be believed that the enemy is responsible for this. Every possible cause of his death is suppressed except one: his membership of the group to which one belongs oneself."[1]

The cause, sanctified by the dead, cannot to be questioned without dishonoring those who gave up their lives. We become enmeshed in the imposed language. When any contradiction is raised or there is a sense that the cause is not just in an absolute sense, the doubts are attacked as apostasy. There is a constant act of remembering and honoring the fallen during war. These ceremonies sanctify the cause. As Americans we speak, following the September attacks, like the Islamic radicals we fight, primarily in clichés. We sound like the Serbian or Croatian nationalists who destroyed the Balkans. The official jargon obscures the game of war—the hunters and the hunted. We accept terms imposed upon us by the state—for example the "war on terror"—and these terms set the narrow parameters by which we are able to think and discuss.

The press, Michael Herr wrote in *Dispatches*, his book on the Vietnam War, "never found a way to report meaningfully about death, which of course was really what it was all about. The most repulsive, transparent gropes for sanctity in the midst of the killing received serious treatment in the papers and on the air. The jargon of the Process got blown into your head like bullets, and by the time you waded through all the Washington stories and all the Saigon stories, all the Other War stories and the corruption stories and the stories about brisk new gains in ARVN effectiveness, the suffering was somehow unimpressive."[2]

It is hard, maybe impossible, to fight a war if the cause is viewed as bankrupt. The sanctity of the cause is crucial to the war effort. The state spends tremendous time protecting, explaining, and promoting the cause. And some of the most important cheerleaders of the cause are the reporters. This is true in nearly every war. During the Gulf War, as in the weeks after the September attacks, communities gathered for vigils and worship services. The enterprise of the state became imbued with a religious aura. We, even those in the press, spoke in the collective. And because we in modern society have walked away from institutions that stand outside the state to find moral guidance and spiritual direction, we turn to the state in times of war. The state and the institutions of state become, for many, the center of worship in wartime. To expose the holes in the myth is to court excommunication.

Edmund Dene Morel, the British crusader against Belgian atrocities in the Congo, denounced World War I as madness.[3] He argued that through a series of treaties kept secret from Parliament and the public, Britain had become caught up in the senseless and tragic debacle. His fight against the war saw mobs break up his meetings with stink bombs and his banners ripped down. He finally could not rent a hall. His friends deserted him. Police raided his office and his home. The wartime censor banned some of his writings. He was flooded with hate mail. The government finally jailed him in 1917. It was only after 8.5 million dead and 21 million wounded that he was proven correct—the treaties did indeed exist. The war indeed was a needless waste. But by then the myth of war was no longer needed, since the fighting had ended.

The moral certitude of the state in wartime is a kind of fundamentalism. And this dangerous messianic brand of religion, one where self-doubt is minimal, has come increasingly to color the modern world of Christianity, Judaism, and Islam. Dr. James Luther Adams, my ethics professor at Harvard Divinity School, used to tell us that we would end our careers fighting an ascendant fundamentalist movement, or, as he liked to say, "the Christian fascists." He was not a scholar to be disregarded, however implausible such a scenario seemed at the time. There is a danger of a growing fusion between those in the state who wage war—both for and against modern states—and those who believe they understand and can act as agents for God.

History is awash with beleaguered revolutionaries and lunatic extremists who were endowed with enough luck and enough ruthlessness to fill power vacuums. The danger is not that fundamentalism will grow so much as that modern, secular society will wither. Already mainstream Christianity, Judaism, and Islam lie defeated and emasculated by the very forces that ironically turned them into tolerant, open institutions. In the event of massive and repeated terrorist strikes or an environmental catastrophe, an authoritarian state church could rise ascendant within American democracy. The current battle between us and our Islamic radical foes can only increase the reach of these groups.

But whether the impetus is ostensibly secular or religious, the adoption of the cause means adoption of the language of the cause. When we speak within the confines of this language we give up our linguistic capacity to question and make moral choices.

The cause is unassailable, wrapped in the mystery reserved for the divine. Those who attempt to expose the fabrications and to unwrap the contradictions of the cause are left isolated and reviled. We did not fight the Persian Gulf War to liberate Kuwait, but to ensure that we would continue to have cheap oil. But oil is hardly a cause that will bring crowds into the street.

I was with young Islamic militants in a Cairo slum a few weeks after the war. They no longer attended the state school because their families did not have the money to hire teachers to tutor them. The teachers, desperate for a decent income, would not let students pass unless they paid. These militants spent their days at the mosque. They saw the Persian Gulf War for what it was, a use of force by a country that consumed 25 percent of the world's petrol to protect its access to cheap oil. The message that was sent to them was this: We have everything and if you try to take it away from us we will kill you. It was not a message I could dispute.

We allied ourselves with some of the most despotic regimes

in the region during the war, including the Syrians, who sponsor an array of terrorist groups. Damascus demanded $3 billion as the price for sending its troops to support the war effort. The morning the invasion began, I traveled with a Marine detachment past the Syrian soldiers. They were drinking tea. They waved us forward. None of them ever saw any fighting. We did not see the Syrian soldiers again until they were passed through our lines after the combat was over so they, and our other Arab allies, could "liberate" Kuwait City. The ecological devastation to the region, the fact that Saddam Hussein remained in power to slaughter thousands of Shiites who rebelled with our encouragement against his regime and then were abandoned by us to their fate, the gross corruption and despotism of the Kuwaiti rulers, who did not move back to Kuwait City until their opulent palaces were refurbished, were minor footnotes to a stage-managed tale of triumph. As in most conflicts, the war, as presented to the public, was fantasy.

When those who commit crimes do so in the name of the cause, they often come to terms with the crimes through an ersatz moral relativism. Facts are trimmed, used, and become as interchangeable as opinions. The Muslims may say the Serbs shelled the marketplace in Sarajevo while the Serbs may say that the Muslims fired shells on their own citizens there to garner international support. Both opinions, if one sits in a café in Belgrade, may be valid. Both the facts and the opinions become a celebration of ignorance, and more ominously, a refusal to discredit the cause that has eaten away at one's moral conscience.

Destruction of honest inquiry, the notion that one fact is as good as the next, is one of the most disturbing consequences of war. The prosecution of war entails lying, often on a massive scale—something most governments engage in but especially when under the duress of war. The Serbs who were eventually able to admit that atrocities were carried out in their name explained away the crimes by saying that everyone did this in war. The same was true among the elite and the military in El Salvador. All could match an atrocity carried out by our side with an atrocity carried out by the enemy. Atrocity canceled out atrocity.

Hannah Arendt noted this attitude in Germany after World War II, calling it "nihilistic relativism." She believed it was a legacy of Nazi propaganda, which, unlike that of non-totalitarian states, was based on the concept that all facts could and would be altered and all Nazi lies should be made to appear true. Reality became a conglomerate of changing circumstances and slogans that could be true one day and false the next.[4]

Illusions punctuate our lives, blinding us to our own inconsistencies and repeated moral failings. But in wartime these illusions are compounded. The cause, the protection of the nation, the fight to "liberate Kuwait" or wage "a war on terrorism," justifies the means. We dismantle our moral universe to serve the cause of war. And once it is dismantled it is nearly impossible to put it back together. It is very hard for most of us to see the justice of the other side, to admit that we too bear guilt. When we are asked to choose between truth and contentment, most of us pick contentment.

Not long after the war in Bosnia, where most human rights monitors blamed the Serbian forces for perhaps 80 percent of the war crimes, a popular film was produced in Serbian called *Pretty Villages, Pretty Flames.* The movie showed images of drunken Bosnian Serb militiamen burning Muslim villages, killing elderly civilians, and carting away truckloads of loot— not a version of the Bosnian war that had been acknowledged until then by many Serbs. Bosnian Serb fighters were portrayed as petty criminals, thugs, and drug addicts. This, to a populace that could still sit around and ask if it were true that Serbian forces shelled Sarajevo, was a revelation.

The film dealt for the first time with the excesses of Bosnian Serb soldiers and the lies of the Serbian nationalist leaders who fueled the war. It was seen as an opening, a frank and candid admission of what really happened. But it was also a classic example of the relativism that worried Arendt. The scramble by some German historians to paint the crimes carried out by Stalin as equivalent to the crimes carried out by Hitler absolved the Germans of responsibility, for all were guilty. And under the guise of candor, this film served the same purpose. It punctured holes in the cause of Serbian nationalism. But it went on to say that one cause was as rotten as the next, that just as the Serbs had been manipulated by their own leaders, so had the Muslims and the Croats. Not only that, the film made sure to bring Tito's Yugoslavia and the international effort to rebuild Bosnia down to the same depraved level.

The failure to dissect the cause of war leaves us open for the next installment. When a cause is exhausted, or no longer needed, it can only be invalidated in direct proportion to the invalidation of the opposing cause. This is a scourge of war. We can deflate our own cause but must deflate the cause of the other as well.

Following the 1995 Dayton peace agreement, the Bosnian Serbs were required to relinquish the suburbs around Sarajevo to the Muslim-led government. A few days before the handover, I stood with a group of ragged Bosnian Serb police officers in blue uniforms. They lined up in a small park and sang. Their voices were barely audible over a scratchy recording of the old anthem of the kingdom of Yugoslavia. The thunder of ammunition exploding in burning buildings drowned out whole stanzas.

The police officers lowered the Bosnian Serb flag from the front of the Grbavica police station, kissed the cloth, and folded it. Milenko Karisik, deputy interior minister for the Bosnian Serbs, proclaimed the officers "heroes" and reminded the few onlookers that the police were the first to raise the rebel Serbian flag in the suburb four years ago.

"We saved this area militarily but we lost it at Dayton," he said. "Maybe this generation of Serbs won't come back, but in future generations the Serbs will return."

The roaring fires in buildings, the bands of drunken Serbs cruising the streets in cars without license plates, and the fear etched on the faces of elderly people who peered through the plastic sheeting nailed across their window frames, illustrated that whatever authority these police officers had wielded disintegrated days ago.

More than a dozen fires sent billows of smoke and flames into a gray, overcast sky. Italian peacekeeping troops, who gunned their armored personnel carriers swiftly through the debris-strewn roads, did little to stop the looting and arson. Of the approximately 60,000 Bosnian Serbs from the five neighborhoods and suburbs that had been scheduled to be turned over to the federation, all but a few thousand had fled.

The repeated explosions came from setting alight the ammunition and grenades that arsonists had planted inside the buildings. Though some of the people who set the fires were vandals, others destroyed their own houses. An elderly Serbian couple who did not want to be identified were driven out of their apartment when a neighbor set his apartment ablaze, setting off explosions.

"What is happening now makes the thought of the Muslims coming here a relief," said the woman, fighting back tears. "We tried so hard to save our apartment. It was all we had in the world."

"People are burning their houses because they are bitter and angry," said Milorad Katić, the mayor of Grbavica. "They don't want to leave their houses for the Muslims to inhabit."

Most of the 2,000 or so Serbs who remained locked the doors of their buildings and barricaded themselves inside their apartments.

When one elderly woman unlocked the front door of her building that afternoon to let in a man who lived there, he brushed her aside and began to dump gasoline in the hallway. She ran desperately outside to find some Italian soldiers who rushed in and prevented the man from starting a fire.

But most were unlucky. I saw two women toss basins of water at a fire on a floor above them, but they soon had to flee as the fire spread.

"We struggled for so long, we endured so much over the last four years," said one woman, "and now we are burned out by our own people."

It was the final act of war, the self-destruction that comes at the end of the campaign of hate and death and violence. I wandered the streets nervously, trying to stay out of the way of drunken groups of armed police who fired rounds into the air. Reporters who had covered the siege of Sarajevo longer than I showed little pity. They muttered that it was what the "Chetniks" deserved, although the victims, from what I could see, were mostly elderly pensioners. This was the apocalyptic end of war, of all wars. The Serbs, like all who are defeated, were consuming themselves.

I made my way to the Vlakovo cemetery and met Nikola Ljesić. He carried with him several yellow candles, a small parcel of food, and a piece of brown wrapping paper filled with nails. He walked past the dun-colored mounds of earth beside several empty graves toward the wooden cross marked with the name of his son, Dragoslav. He said that the eighteen-year-old had been shot dead by a Muslim sniper in June 1992.

He kissed the cross. He knelt and kissed the dirt on the grave. He removed his brown wool hat and stood in silence.

"I would like to take him in my arms one more time, and kiss him and hold him," he said.

Ljesić lit the candles in front of his son's grave. He watched the flames flicker in the cold wind that whipped down from the barren, brown hills around him. On a weathered wooden bench he laid out two loaves of bread, a shaker of salt, smoked pork, a bottle of brandy, and a shot glass. The two grave diggers next to him, wearing blue work shirts over worn sweaters, ate the bread with salt and a piece of meat. They quickly downed the alcohol.

When the graveside mourning ritual was completed, Ljesić nodded for the men to begin hacking through the frigid earth until they reached the remains of his youngest child.

"I took a handful of tranquilizers before I came," he said.

"You don't know these Muslim fanatics," Ljesić said. "They have no morality. They would dig up my son and take his bones and burn them."

Cemetery officials were drawing up plans to unearth the some 1,000 dead who had been killed in the war and move all the bodies to a new cemetery in Sokolac, outside of Pale, the headquarters of the Bosnian Serbs.

"We only have three workers," said Jovo Kuljanin, the director of the cemetery, "so people often have to dig up their own graves. We don't have any hearses; people have to arrange for their own transportation. And everyone who wants a metal coffin must pay $140 for it. We can't provide one."

Ljesić, who had last visited the grave on January 9, his son's birthday, was unable to pay for a metal coffin. Instead he brought plastic sheeting, handed out by the United Nations High Commissioner for Refugees to cover windows. In the pocket of his black suit he carried nails to pound the coffin back together. He had paid Srdjan Manojlovic $70 to carry the coffin to Sokolac in his 1987 red Yugoslav Zastava van.

The war had shattered Ljesić's life. His two daughters left Bosnia—one for Germany and the other for France. His wife, whom he had not been able to contact for three years, was cut off from him in Muslim-held Sarajevo. His home, on the outskirts of the city, had been blasted into rubble. He had lost his job and lived alone in a small apartment in Doboj. Yet, even as he dug up the body of his son, he could not face the perfidiousness of what he had once supported. He knew it was rotten. He knew it was waste. He was in deep despair, but always the Muslim enemy loomed above him, ready to violate the dead, his dead. No matter how horrible his own war was, no matter how corrupt and brutal his own leaders were, the cause could be justified if only by a negative, by the fear of the other.

"My wife does not know I am here today," he said. "She was not allowed by the Muslims to come to our son's funeral. She has never visited his grave. It would kill her to see this now."

Milivoje Matić, a burly man in a brown coat, stopped to take a shot of brandy and express his condolences to Ljesić. He listened patiently to the story of how the boy was killed. Matić told the story of his brother, Slobodan, who he said had been tortured to death in a Muslim jail in Sarajevo.

He then went to work a few feet away, swinging a pickax over his head to dig up his brother's grave.

Small beads of sweat collected on his forehead.

"His children called and asked me to get the body," he said breathlessly. "They asked me to dig him up."

When the coffin containing the remains of Ljesić's son was uncovered, the grave diggers brought in a small backhoe to lift it out of the ground. As it was hoisted up, the dilapidated brown-painted wooden box spewed water into the hole.

Ljesić removed his hat. He pulled the nails from his pocket.

"We can put it back together," he said softly to Zeljko Kneževic, one of the grave diggers. "Please do it for me. I will give you all the money I have. It is not a lot, but it is all that is left."

Kneževic pounded nails into the three planks of wood that once formed the lid. The corpse, wrapped in a gray, damp blanket, faced the open sky. Ljesić, as if he were putting his son to bed, gently laid a clean blanket over the remains. An American Chinook helicopter passed overhead.

"I will put this plastic around the coffin," he explained to the gravediggers. "We will tie it up with string."

When the coffin was repaired, Ljesić embraced Kneževic.

"I will never forget what you did for me," the father said.

The end of the coffin, covered with the milky white plastic sheeting, stuck out from the back of the van as it drove away.

Kneževic, seated on another grave, lit a cigarette.

"We have to do five graves tomorrow," he said. "I was here when they put the first body in the ground. It looks like I will be here when they pull the last one out. When the cemetery is empty, my job will be done and I will leave with everyone else."

7

EROS AND THANATOS

Beyond all this, the wish to be alone
However the sky grows dark with invitation-cards
However we follow the printed directions of sex
However the family is photographed under the
flagstaff—
Beyond all this, the wish to be alone

Beneath it all desire of oblivion runs
Despite the artful tensions of the calendar,
The life insurance, the tabled fertility rites,
The costly aversion of the eyes from death —
Beneath it all desire of oblivion runs.

•

PHILIP LARKIN

DURING THE WAR IN EL SALVADOR I WORKED WITH A
photographer who had a slew of close calls and then
called it quits. He moved to Miami. He took pictures of tepid
domestic stories for one of the newsweeklies. But life in Florida
was flat, dull, uninteresting. He could not adjust and soon came
back. From the moment he stepped off the plane it was clear he

had returned to die. Just as there are some soldiers or war correspondents who seem to us immortal and whose loss comes as a sobering reminder that death has no favorites, there are also those in war who are locked in a grim embrace with death from which they cannot escape. He was frightening to behold, a walking corpse. He was shot a few months later through the back in a firefight. It took him less than a minute to die.

Sigmund Freud divided the forces in human nature between the Eros instinct, the impulse within us that propels us to become close to others, to preserve and conserve, and the Thanatos, or death instinct, the impulse that works towards the annihilation of all living things, including ourselves. For Freud these forces were in eternal conflict. He was pessimistic about ever eradicating war. All human history, he argued, is a tug-of-war between these two instincts.

"The meaning of the evolution of civilization is no longer obscure to us," Freud wrote in *Civilization and Its Discontents*. "It must present the struggle between Eros and Death, between the instinct of life and the instinct of destruction, as it works itself out in the human species. This struggle is what all life essentially consists of."[1]

We believe in the nobility and self-sacrifice demanded by war, especially when we are blinded by the narcotic of war. We discover in the communal struggle, the shared sense of meaning and purpose, a cause. War fills our spiritual void. I do not miss war, but I miss what it brought. I can never say I was happy in the midst of the fighting in El Salvador, or Bosnia, or Kosovo, but I had a sense of purpose, of calling. And this is a quality war shares with love, for we are, in love, also able to choose fealty and self-sacrifice over security.

Happiness is elusive and protean. And it is sterile when

devoid of meaning. But meaning, when it is set in the vast arena of war with its high stakes, its adrenaline-driven rushes, its bold sweeps and drama, is heartless and self-destructive. The initial selflessness of war mirrors that of love, the chief emotion war destroys. And this is what war often looks and feels like, at its inception: love. The ancient Greeks understood this strange relationship between love and death in wartime. When Achilles kills Penthesilea, the queen of the Amazons, in the Trojan War, he falls in love with her as she expires on the battlefield. Once she is dead, once love is dead, Achilles is doomed.

We are tempted to reduce life to a simple search for happiness. Happiness, however, withers if there is no meaning. The other temptation is to disavow the search for happiness in order to be faithful to that which provides meaning. But to live only for meaning—indifferent to all happiness—makes us fanatic, self-righteous, and cold. It leaves us cut off from our own humanity and the humanity of others. We must hope for grace, for our lives to be sustained by moments of meaning and happiness, both equally worthy of human communion.

During the first phases of the war in Kosovo I moved about the countryside in an armored jeep. I slept in wooden sheds and barns or on the floors of peasant homes. One bitterly cold winter morning I woke at first light in a hut. I watched the wind blow snow through the slates over my sleeping bag. I heard from local rebels about a Serb attack on a nearby village. The victims would be buried in a few hours. As so often happened, I had to leave my vehicle behind because of the extensive Serb roadblocks. I walked to the site on foot. It was, as usual, a perilous game of cat-and-mouse, one I had played for five years with the military in El Salvador. During the funeral Serb snipers opened fire on the crowd. We darted for cover. I filed my story,

quickly typed out and sent over the satellite phone I carried in
my backpack. Then I walked out. To record the atrocities, even
as I knew the killings would continue, was my task. But by then
it was destroying me. I felt profoundly alone.

In the wake of catastrophe, including the attacks of September 11, 2001, there is a desperate longing by all those affected to
be in the physical presence of those they love. When a heavy
shell landed in Sarajevo, or an assassination took place in the
streets of San Salvador, or a suicide bomber blew himself up
in Jerusalem, mothers, fathers, husbands, wives, and children
pawed through the onlookers seeking physical reunification
with those they loved. This love, like death, radiates outwards. It
battles Thanatos at the very moment of death's sting. These
two fundamental human impulses crash like breakers into each
other. And however much beyond reason, there is always a feeling that love is not powerless or impotent as we had believed a
few seconds before. Love alone fuses happiness and meaning.
Love alone can fight the impulse that lures us toward self-
destruction.

The question is whether America now courts death. We no
longer seem chastened by war as we were in the years after the
Vietnam War. The Bush administration has revised its "Nuclear
Posture Review" to give us "more flexible nuclear strike capa-
bilities." Washington wants "more options" with which to confront contingencies "immediate, potential and unexpected," for
smaller but more effective mega-tonnages to be deployed. This
flirtation with weapons of mass destruction is a flirtation with
our own obliteration, an embrace again of Thanatos.

There are few sanctuaries in war. But one is provided by couples in love. They are not able to staunch the slaughter. They are
often powerless and can themselves often become victims. But

it was with them, seated around a wood stove, usually over a simple meal, that I found sanity and was reminded of what it means to be human. Love kept them grounded. It was to such couples that I retreated during the wars in Central America, the Middle East, and the Balkans. Love, when it is deep and sustained by two individuals, includes self-giving—often self-sacrifice—as well as desire. For the covenant of love is such that it recognizes both the fragility and the sanctity of the individual. It recognizes itself in the other. It alone can save us.

I did not sleep well in war. I could rarely recall my dreams, waking only to know that they had been harsh and violent. When I left the war zones, the nightmares descended on me like furies. I had horrible visions of war. I would dream of being in combat with my father or young son and unable to protect them. But I could sleep in the homes of such couples. Their love spread a protective blanket over us. It was able to blot out the war, although the lure of combat, the distant rattle of automatic weapons beckoned us back, and we always went.

Aristotle said that only two living entities are capable of complete solitude and complete separateness: God and beast. Because of this the most acute form of suffering for human beings is loneliness. The isolated individual can never be adequately human. And many of war's most fervent adherents are those atomized individuals who, before the war came, were profoundly alone and unloved. They found fulfillment in war, perhaps because it was the closest they came to love. If we do not acknowledge such an attraction, which is, in some ways, so akin to love, we can never combat it.

We are all tempted to honor false covenants of race, nationalism, class, and gender. They sometimes compete for our loyalty. War, of course, is often—maybe always—a false covenant.

Sham covenants are based on exclusion rather than universality. All covenants that lack an adequate sense of humility and an acknowledgment of the sinfulness of our own cause are false covenants. The prophets warned us about them.

The cost of war is often measured in the physical destruction of a country's infrastructure, in the blasted buildings, factories, and bridges, in the number of dead. But probably worse is the psychological and spiritual toll. This cost takes generations to heal. It cripples and perverts whole societies, as Europe saw with the shattered veterans from World War I. But even for those who know the cost of war, it still holds out the promise of eradicating the thorny problems of life.

In the beginning war looks and feels like love. But unlike love it gives nothing in return but an ever-deepening dependence, like all narcotics, on the road to self-destruction. It does not affirm but places upon us greater and greater demands. It destroys the outside world until it is hard to live outside war's grip. It takes a higher and higher dose to achieve any thrill. Finally, one ingests war only to remain numb. The world outside war becomes, as Freud wrote, "uncanny." The familiar becomes strangely unfamiliar—many who have been in war find this when they return home. The world we once understood and longed to return to stands before us as alien, strange, and beyond our grasp.

In 1999 the British journalist Anthony Loyd published *My War Gone By, I Miss It So*, a book about his twin addictions to heroin and to the war in Bosnia. His account illuminates the self-destruction impulse that is fed by war and drugs as well as the highs that propel many into combat. For Loyd, like Michael Herr, war was the ultimate drug experience. It was the chance to taste extremes that would, he hoped, bring about a catharsis or obliteration. In times of peace, drugs are war's pale substitute. But drugs, in the end, cannot compare with the awful power and rush of battle. This was not why I went to war, but the twisted voyeurism and narcotic of war Loyd described attracted many to the battlefields and held them there.

> Deep down I was aware at the time that many of my moti-vations were fairly dark. On one level my sense of despair had been dispelled by therapy, yet on another it had not been replaced by either the desire for a future or the concept of one. I felt more aware of who I was, but that in itself—dominated as it was by sensations of fragmentation and iso-lation—filled me with no great hope, and in many ways only fueled an appetite for destruction.[2]

There are those for whom violence is sexual. They carry their phallic weapons slung low at an angle toward the ground. Most of these fighters are militiamen, those who stay away from real combat, have little training or discipline, and primarily terrorize the weak and defenseless. And they look the part, often with tight black fatigues, wraparound sunglasses, and big ugly jeeps or cars with tinted windows. For them war is about empower-ment. They have turned places like the Congo into Hobbesian playgrounds.

These warlords rise to power with gangs who prey on minorities and the weak. When they are done, they turn on those they were fighting to protect. I was in the Bosnian Serb town of Banja Luka in the summer of 1995 not long after Ser-bian militias had driven out most of the ethnic Croats. Once the militias had finished looting the homes of the ethnic Croats and stealing their cars, they set up roadblocks to steal cars from the

Serbs who lived in the city. The cars were then driven over the border into Serbia for sale.

When the mask of war slips away and the rot and corruption is exposed, when the addiction turns sour and rank, when the myth is exposed as a fraud, we feel soiled and spent. It is then that we sink into despair, a despair that can lead us to welcome death. This despair is more common than many expect.

In the 1973 Arab-Israeli war, almost a third of all Israeli casualties were due to psychiatric causes, and the war lasted only a few weeks. A World War II study determined that after sixty days of continuous combat, 98 percent of all surviving soldiers will have become psychiatric casualties. They found that a common trait among the 2 percent who were able to endure sustained combat was a predisposition toward "aggressive psychopathic personalities."[3]

During the war in El Salvador soldiers could serve in the army for three or four years or longer, virtually until they psychologically collapsed. In garrison towns commanders banned the sale of sedatives because of abuse by troops. In this war the emotionally maimed were common.

Edilberto Ayala, a nineteen-year-old Salvadoran army sergeant, spent five years fighting, and suddenly lost his vision after his unit walked into a rebel ambush. The rebels killed eleven soldiers in the firefight, including Ayala's closest friend. A couple dozen soldiers were wounded. He was unable to see again until he was placed in an army hospital.

"I have these horrible headaches," he told me, sitting on the edge of his hospital bed. "There is shrapnel in my head. I keep telling the doctors to take it out."

But the doctors told me he had no head wounds.

J. Glenn Gray, a World War II combat veteran who taught

philosophy after the war, wrote: "Few of us can hold on to our real selves long enough to discover the real truths about ourselves and this whirling earth to which we cling. This is especially true of men in war. The great god Mars tries to blind us when we enter his realm, and when we leave he gives us a generous cup of the waters of Lethe to drink."[4]

This self-deception is powerful. It propels those in war forward. When it falls away, when we grasp war's reality, a universe collapses. Many of those who suddenly perceive the raw brutality and lie of war crumble into heaps.

Jon Steele, a cameraman who spent years in war zones, had a nervous breakdown in a crowded Heathrow Airport in 1994 after returning from Sarajevo, when for a moment he saw the cold reality of what he was doing, a reality that stripped away the self-righteous gloss and addiction to battle.

"I came back from Sarajevo," he said in an interview in the Israeli newspaper *Ha'aretz*. "We were in a place called Sniper's Alley, and I filmed a girl there who had been hit in the neck by a sniper's bullet. I filmed her dying in the ambulance and only after she was dead, I suddenly understood that the last thing she had seen was the reflection of the lens of the camera I was holding in front of her face. This wiped me out. I grabbed the camera and I started running down Snipers' Alley, filming at knee level the Bosnians running from place to place. I think that I broke down because I got things backward—I thought that because I was trying to be a hero and get exclusive pictures, people were dying."[5]

War is necrophilia. And this necrophilia is central to soldiering, just as it is central to the makeup of suicide bombers and terrorists. The necrophilia is hidden under platitudes about duty or comradeship. It waits, especially in moments when we seem to have little to live for and no hope, or in moments when the intoxication of war is at its pitch, to be unleashed. When we spend long enough in war it comes to us as a kind of release, a fatal and seductive embrace that can consummate the long flirtation in war with our own destruction. The ancient Greeks had a word for such a drive. They called it *ekpyrosis*—to be consumed by a ball of fire. They used the word to describe heroes.

War throws us into a frenzy in which all human life, including our own, seems secondary. The atavism of war creates us in war's image. In Chuck Sudetic's book *Blood and Vengeance* the former reporter for *The New York Times* writes of how he was eventually overpowered by the culture of death in wartime:

> I once walked through a town littered with the purple-and-yellow bodies of men and women and a few children, some shot to death, some with their heads torn off, and I felt nothing; I strolled around with a photographer, scratched notes, and lifted sheets covering the bodies of dead men to see if they had been castrated; I picked up a white flag from the ground near the twisted bodies of half a dozen men in civilian clothes who had been shot next to a wall, and then I carried the flag home and hung it above my desk. I once saw soldiers unload babies crushed to death in the back of a truck and immediately ran off to interview their mothers. I accidentally killed an eighteen-year-old man who raced in front of my car on a bike; his head was smashed; I held the door when they loaded him into the backseat of the automobile that carried him to the emergency room of Sarajevo's main hospital; I expressed my condolences to his father; then I got a tow back to my hotel, went to my room, and sent that day's story to New York.[6]

In Milovan Djilas's memoir of the partisan war in Yugo-slavia, he too wrote of the enticement death held for the com-batants. He stood over the body of his comrade, the commander Sava Kovačević, and found that

> Dying did not seem terrible or unjust. This was the most extraordinary, the most exalted moment of my life: death did not seem strange or undesirable. That I restrained myself from charging blindly into the fray and death, was perhaps due to my sense of obligation to the troops, or to some com-rade's reminder concerning the tasks at hand. In my memory I returned to those moments many times, with the same feel-ing of intimacy with death and desire for it, while I was in prison, particularly during my first incarceration.[7]

War ascendant wipes out Eros. It wipes out all delicacy and tenderness. And this is why those in war swing from rank sen-timentality to perversion, with little in between. Stray puppies, street kids, cats, anything that can be an object of affection for soldiers are adopted and pampered even in the midst of killing, the beating and torture of prisoners, and the razing of villages. If the pets die they are buried with elaborate rituals and little grave markers. But it is not only love, although the soldiers insist it feels like love. These animals, as well as the young waifs who collect around military units, are total dependents. They pay homage to the absolute power above them. Indeed, it may be that at times they please or they die.

In the midst of slaughter the only choice is often between hate and lust. Human beings become objects, objects to extin-guish or to provide carnal gratification. The widespread casual and frenetic sex in wartime often crosses the line into perversion and violence. It exposes the vast moral void. When life becomes worth nothing, when one is not sure of survival, when a society is ruled by fear, there often seems only death or fleeting, carnal pleasure. This is why Lady Ann in Shakespeare's *Richard III* goes to Richard's bed. She sleeps with Richard because her moral universe has been destroyed. This kind of love is the product of the impersonal violence of war.

In war we may deform ourselves, our essence, by subverting passion, loyalty, and love to duty. Perhaps one could argue that this is why Virgil's Aeneas appears so woefully unhappy in *The Aeneid*. Despite his love for Dido he must leave her to found the empire in Italy: *hic amor, haec patria est*—there is my love, there my country. Yet in moments of extremity to make a moral choice, to defy war's enticement, to defend love, can be self-destructive. Shakespeare shows it in Antony in *Antony and Cleopatra*, as he does in the final defeat of Coriolanus. Antony embraces love and passion and loses empire. Like Dido, by giving himself to love, he dooms his empire and cuts his life short. He is no match for Octavius's bloodless thirst for power.

In the rise to power we become smaller, power absorbs us, and once power is attained we are often its pawn. As in *Richard III*, the all-powerful prince, can swiftly fall prey to the forces he thought he had harnessed. So too in war. Shakespeare's Lear and Richard III gain knowledge only as they are pushed down the ladder, as they are stripped of all illusions. Love may not always triumph, but it keeps us human. It offers the only chance to escape from the contagion of war. Perhaps it is the only antidote. And there are times when remaining human is the only victory possible.

Kurt Schork, a Reuters correspondent who spent a decade in war zones before being killed in an ambush in Sierra Leone, wrote a story out of Sarajevo about Bosko Brckić, a Serb, and

Admira Ismić, a Muslim, both twenty-five. They had been sweethearts since high school. The lovers tried to flee the besieged city in May 1993, a year after the war started, but were gunned down by Serb snipers.

They died together on the banks of Sarajevo's Miljacka River. Bosko fell dead instantly. Admira was badly wounded. She crawled over and hugged him. She expired in his arms. Bosko lay face-down on the pavement, his right arm bent awkwardly behind him. Admira lay next to him, her left arm across his back. Another corpse, that of a man shot five months earlier, lay decomposing nearby.

Their bodies lay there for four days, sprawled near the Vrbana bridge, a pitted wasteland of shell-blasted rubble, downed tree branches, and dangling power lines, before they were recovered.

They are buried together, under a heart-shaped headstone, in the Lion's Cemetery for the victims of the war. Kurt is buried next to them. Kurt, brilliant, courageous, and driven, had been unable to break free from the addiction of war. His entrapment, his long flirtation with Thanatos, was never mentioned at the memorial service staged for him in Washington by the Reuters bureaucrats he did not respect. Everyone tiptoed around it. But those of us who knew him understood that he had been consumed by his addiction. I had worked with Kurt for ten years, starting in northern Iraq. Literate, funny—it seems the brave are often funny—he and I passed books back and forth in our struggle to make sense of the madness around us. His loss was a hole that will never be filled.

I flew to Sarajevo and met the British filmmaker Dan Reed. It was an overcast November day. We stood over the grave and downed a pint of whiskey. Dan lit a candle. I recited a poem the Roman lyric poet Catullus had written to honor his dead brother.

By strangers' coasts and waters, many days at sea,
I come here for the rites of your unworlding,
Bringing for you, the dead, these last gifts of the living
And my words—vain sounds for the man of dust.
Alas, my brother,
You have been taken from me. You have been taken from me,
By cold chance turned a shadow, and my pain.
Here are the foods of the old ceremony, appointed
Long ago for the starvelings under the earth:
Take them: your brother's tears have made them wet; and take
Into eternity my hail and my farewell.[8]

It was there, among a few thousand war dead, that Kurt
belonged. He died because he could not free himself war, from
the death impulse. He was in Africa searching for new highs. He
was trying to replicate what he had found in Sarajevo. But he
could not. War could never be new again. I had tried for years
after El Salvador to make it come back. It was never the same.
Kurt had been in East Timor and Chechnya. Sierra Leone, I
was sure, meant little to him. Miguel Gil Morano, a Spanish
cameraman, who had also covered the wars in Bosnia and
Kosovo, died with him. They were, like all who do not let go,
consumed by a ball of fire. But they lit the fuse. And they would
be the first to admit it.

Viktor Frankl, in *Man's Search for Meaning*, writes of the grim
battle between love and Thanatos in Auschwitz. He recalls
being on a work detail, freezing in the blast of the Polish winter,
when he began to think about his wife, who had already been
gassed, although he did not know this at the time.

A thought transfixed me: for the first time in my life I saw
the truth as it is set into song by so many poets, proclaimed

as the final wisdom by so many thinkers. The truth—that love is the ultimate and the highest goal to which man can aspire. Then I grasped the meaning of the greatest secret that human poetry and human thought and belief have to impart: The salvation of man is through love and in love.[9]

The Thanatos instinct is a drive toward suicide, individual and collective. War celebrates only power—and we come to believe in wartime that it is the only real form of power. It preys on our most primal and savage impulses. It allows us to do what peacetime society forbids or restrains us from doing. It allows us to kill. However much soldiers regret killing once it is finished, however much they spend their lives trying to cope with the experience, the act itself, fueled by fear, excitement, the pull of the crowd, and the god-like exhilaration of destroying, is often thrilling.

I have watched fighters in El Salvador, Nicaragua, Guatemala, the Sudan, the Punjab, Iraq, Bosnia, and Kosovo enter villages, tense, exhausted, wary of ambushes, with the fear and tension that comes from combat, and begin to shoot at random. Flames soon lick up from houses. Discipline, if there was any, disintegrates. Items are looted, civilians are battered with rifle butts, units fall apart, and the violence directed toward unarmed men, women, and children grows as it feeds on itself. The eyes of the soldiers who carry this orgy of death are crazed. They speak only in guttural shouts. They are high on the power to spare lives or take them, the divine power to destroy. And they are indeed, for a moment, gods swatting down powerless human beings like flies. The lust for violence, the freedom to eradicate the world around them, even human lives, is seductive. And the line that divides us, who would like to see ourselves as civilized and compassionate, from such communal barbarity is razor-thin. In wartime it often seems to matter little where one came from or how well-schooled and moral one was before the war began. The frenzy of the crowd is overpowering.

Bob Kerrey, a former United States senator who won the Medal of Honor for his military service in Vietnam, once led a combat mission that caused the deaths of thirteen to twenty unarmed civilians, most of them women and children. When this story was first revealed in the spring of 2001, there was, among an unknowing public, an expression of shock and an effort to explain such behavior. But the revelation was, rather than an anomaly, an example of how most wars are fought. It was a glimpse into the reality of war that many in the public, anxious not to see war's sordid nature, worked hard to shut. Kerrey, in a speech at the Virginia Military Institute soon after the incident was made public, said: "I have been haunted by it for thirty-two years."

The raid, which took place in 1969, saw Kerrey, then a twenty-five-year-old lieutenant who had arrived in Vietnam a month earlier, lead a group of six Navy Seals—the informal name for Sea-Air-Land units—behind enemy lines. They hoped to capture a Vietcong leader who was reported to be holding a meeting that night. The unit was ferried to the spot by boat. They encountered a thatched hut and killed those inside. There were, those in the unit said, women inside. They ran into more huts. More women and children were killed, although Kerrey says he and his men came under fire. "The thing that I will remember until the day I die is walking in and finding, I don't know, 14 or so, I don't even know that the number was, women and children, who were dead," he told *The New York Times Magazine*.[10]

In an interview with *The Wall Street Journal*, Kerrey said, "This is killing me. I'm tired of people describing me as a hero and holding this inside."[11]

The military histories—which tell little of war's reality—crowd out the wrenching tales by the emotionally maimed. Each generation again responds to war as innocents. Each generation discovers its own disillusionment—often after a terrible price. The myth of war and the drug of war wait to be tasted. The mythical heroes of the past loom over us. Those who can tell us the truth are silenced or prefer to forget. The state needs the myth, as much as it needs its soldiers and its machines of war, to survive.

To say the least, killing is nearly always a sordid affair. Those who carry such memories do so with difficulty, even when the cause seems just. Moreover, those who are killed do not die the clean death we see on television or film. They die messy, disturbing deaths that often plague the killers. And the bodies of the newly slain retain a disquieting power. The rows of impersonal dead, stacked like firewood one next to the other, draped on roadsides, twisted into strange, often grimly humorous shapes, speak. I have looked into the open eyes of dead men and wished them shut, for they seemed to beckon me into the underworld. You will be me, the eyes call out, see what you will become. Even hardened soldiers drape cloth over such faces or reach out and push the eyelids shut. The eyes of the dead are windows into a world we fear.

Goodbye Darkness, William Manchester's memoir of the Pacific war in World War II, has an unvarnished account of what it feels like to shoot another man. Nothing is more sickening in war than watching human lives get snuffed out. Nothing haunts you more. And it is never, as outsiders think, clean or easy or neat. Killing is a dirty business, more like butchering animals.

Manchester describes, in the opening pages of his memoir, the only time he shot a Japanese soldier he could see.

Not only was he the first Japanese soldier I had ever shot at; he was the only one I had seen at close quarters. He was a robin-fat, moon-faced, roly-poly little man with his thick, stubby, trunk-like legs sheathed in faded khaki puttees and the rest of him squeezed into a uniform that was much too tight. Unlike me, he was wearing a tin hat, dressed to kill. But I was quite safe from him. His Arisaka rifle was strapped on in a sniper's harness, and though he had heard me, and was trying to turn toward me, the harness sling had him trapped. He couldn't disentangle himself from it. His eyes were rolling in panic. Realizing that he couldn't extricate his arms and defend himself, he was backing toward a corner with a curious, crablike motion.

My first shot had missed him, embedding itself in the straw wall, but the second caught him dead-on in the femoral artery. His left thigh blossomed, swiftly turning to mush. A wave of blood gushed from the wound; then another boiled out, sheeting across his legs, pooling on the earthen floor. Mutely he looked down at it. He dipped a hand in it and listlessly smeared his cheek red. His shoulders gave a little spasmodic jerk, as though someone had whacked him on the back; then he emitted a tremendous, raspy fart, slumped down, and died. I kept firing, wasting government property. Already I thought I detected the dark brown effluvium of the freshly slain, a sour, pervasive emanation which is different from anything you have known. Yet seeing death as this range, like smelling it, requires no previous experience. You instantly recognize it the spastic convulsion and the rattle, which in his case was not loud, but deprecating and conciliatory, like the manners of the civilian Japanese. He continued to sink until he reached the earthen floor. His eyes glazed over. Almost immediately a fly landed on his left eyeball. It was joined by another. I don't know how long I stood there staring. I knew from previous combat what lay ahead for the corpse. It would swell, the bloat, bursting out of the uniform. Then the face would turn from yellow to red, to purple, to green, to black. My father's account of the Argonne had omitted certain vital facts. A feeling of disgust and self-hatred clotted darkly in my throat, gagging me.

Jerking my head to shake off the stupor, I slipped a new, fully loaded magazine into the butt of my .45. Then I began to tremble, and next to shake, all over. I sobbed, in a voice still grainy with fear: "I'm sorry." Then I threw up all over myself. I recognized the half-digested C-ration beans dribbling down my front, smelled the vomit above the cordite. At the same time I noticed another odor; I had urinated in my skivvies. I pondered fleetly why our excretions become so loathsome the instant they leave the body. Then Barney burst in on me, his carbine at the ready, his face gray, as though he, not I, had just become a partner in the firm of death. He ran over to the Nip's body, grabbed its stacking swivel—its neck—and let go, satisfied that it was a cadaver. I marveled at his courage; I couldn't have taken a step toward that corner. He approached me and then backed away in revulsion, from my foul stench. He said: "Slim, you stink." I said nothing. I knew I had become a thing of tears and twitchings and dirtied pants. I remember wondering dumbly: Is that what they mean by "conspicuous gallantry"?[12]

There is among many who fight in war a sense of shame, one that is made worse by the patriotic drivel used to justify the act of killing in war. Those who seek meaning in patriotism do not want to hear the truth of war, wary of bursting the bubble. The tensions between those who were there and those who were not, those who refuse to let go of the myth and those that know it to be a lie feed into the dislocation and malaise after war. In the end, neither side cares to speak to the other. The shame and alienation of combat soldiers, coupled with the indifference to the truth of war by those who were not there, reduces many societies to silence. It seems better to forget.

"I, too, belong to this species," J. Glenn Gray wrote. "I am ashamed not only of my own deeds, not only of my nation's deeds, but of human deeds as well. I am ashamed to be a man."[13]

When Ernie Pyle, the American war correspondent in World War II, was killed on the Pacific island of Ie Shima in 1945, a rough draft of a column was found on his body. He was preparing it for release upon the end of the war in Europe. He had done much to promote the myth of the warrior and the heroism of soldiering, but by the end he seemed to tire of it all.

But there are many of the living who have had burned into their brains forever the unnatural sight of cold dead men scattered over the hillsides and in the ditches along the high rows of hedge throughout the world.

Dead men by mass production—in one country after another—month after month and year after year. Dead men in winter and dead men in summer.

Dead men in such familiar promiscuity that they become monotonous.

Dead men in such monstrous infinity that you come

almost to hate them. These are the things that you at home need not even try to understand. To you at home they are columns of figures, or he is a near one who went away and just didn't come back. You didn't see him lying so grotesque and pasty beside the gravel road in France.

We saw him, saw him by the multiple thousands. That's the difference.[14]

Discarded veterans are never a pretty sight. They are troubled and some physically maimed. They often feel betrayed, misunderstood and alone. It is hard to integrate again into peacetime society. Many are shunted aside, left to nuture their resentment and pain.

I found Kazem Ahangaron in Naushahr, on Iran's Caspian coast, not long after the end of the eight-year war with Iraq. He was once a disciple of war. But the violence he turned on Iraqi soldiers he had turned against himself.

"I tried to do it with pills, Valium and depressants, mostly," the gaunt twenty-eight-year-old veteran said, seated on a white pebble beach. "They pumped my stomach out at the hospital. But twelve of my friends have killed themselves this year."

The Caspian resort city, skirted by jagged mountains and towering fir trees, was once the summer capital of the shah. Its faded yet elegant whitewashed villas belonged to the officials of the monarchy before the 1979 Islamic revolution.

When I visited the seedy remains of Naushahr it had one of the highest rates of suicides in Iran, most by unemployed and disillusioned veterans of the war with Iraq. Figures in Iran are hard to come by and often unreliable, but doctors in the city told me that there had been 400 suicides of the town's 80,000 people in the past year. The men, out of work and alienated from the puritanical rule of the clerics, were unable to find a home or marry. They looked back on the raw carnage of the war with bitterness and ahead with despair. Drugs took the place of battle. Suicide took the place of heroic death.

Many of the suicides in Naushahr were caused by Phostoxin, small phosphate tablets known as "rice pills" that were used in granaries to kill insects. The tablets would paralyze the nervous system and send the young men into a coma. The city did not have a psychiatrist. Many rice merchants, in an effort to curb the suicides, had stopped selling the German-made tablets.

The Islamic clerics who took over Iran sought to reshape the country into a nation of devout Muslims. They spurned the decadence of the West, including what the clerics condemned as the West's loose sexual mores, drug use, and thirst for sensual gratification.

Naushahr's dance halls and bars had been turned over to shopkeepers or boarded over. The beaches were segregated by sex and patrolled by squads of morality police. At the crest of a hill, the lavish Chinese Horse casino, which once glittered through the night like a huge ocean liner, lay in rubble.

But rather than build a new generation of believers, the fundamentalist leaders created a generation of men who were alienated and infected with the hopeless despair of war and violence.

"Life has became a charade," Ahangaron said. "We carry out one life in public and another in private."

The war, once, captured their imaginations. But the years of slaughter had left them listless and addicted to hashish and opium. Many were volunteers who believed that they were not only defending their nation but helping to create a new society in the war with Iraq. The disillusionment was total.

"Iran's best wrestlers come from Naushahr," said Ramazan Gharib, a thirty-five-year-old veteran, "and the army recruiters, very cleverly, used this. When the war started we were all exhorted to show our strength, our manliness, and we went down to enlist."

But the front lines, where Iranian units were butchered en masse as they tried to sweep in human waves across the mud flats, held little glory. And many who survived the war, which began in 1980 and ended in 1988, returned changed and unsettled by the senseless carnage.

The town's leading cleric, Mohammed Masha Yekhi, had called on young people to chose life rather than suicide. He said he would not allow those who committed suicide a Muslim burial.

I sat one morning with two war veterans on the porch of a dilapidated villa overlooking the Caspian. The men, who fished and used their boats to take people water skiing, were slumped in wicker chairs drinking cups of sweet tea.

The two men told me that they had easy access to the drugs, homemade beer, and grain alcohol that was sold on the beach. They smuggled out tins of caviar from the state-run packaging plant and traded it with Russian sailors, anchored offshore, for vodka. For a price they guided couples to secluded beaches, where women could swim in bathing suits and embrace their boyfriends, activities the clerics had forbidden. The money they earned was swallowed by their addiction.

"I will never be normal again," said one of the men, who spent twenty-three months at the front. "I am nervous. I can't control my anger. If anything disturbs me, like a minor car accident, I explode."

The second man, who was a lieutenant in the war, looked out

over the water and said in a monotone, "My battalion was ordered across the flats early one morning. Within a couple of hours 400 soldiers were dead and hundreds more wounded. It was a stupid, useless waste. When we got back they called us traitors."

In the shade of a stone wall, just in front of the villa, with its collection of drooping cots and dirty shag carpets, a young man, dressed in a black shirt and pants, stared blankly at the water.

"He comes here every day," one of the veterans said. "He just finished his army service, but he has no job and nowhere to go. He smokes hash and watches the surf."

The men said they lived on the margins of existence, sometimes sleeping under grass-roofed huts. The pittance the men earned, the psychological burdens they bore, and their inability to afford a place to live had crushed them.

"All we have left is the sea," a former officer said, "and the sea is what keeps us here. But then one day even the sea isn't enough."

As long as we think abstractly, as long as we find in patriotism and the exuberance of war our fulfillment, we will never understand those who do battle against us, or how we are perceived by them, or finally those who do battle for us and how we should respond to it all. We will never discover who we are. We will fail to confront the capacity we all have for violence. And we will court our own extermination. By accepting the facile cliché that the battle under way against terrorism is a battle against evil, by easily branding those who fight us as the barbarians, we, like them, refuse to acknowledge our own culpability. We ignore real injustices that have led many of those arrayed against us to their rage and despair.

Late one night, unable to sleep during the war in El Salvador, I picked up Shakespeare's *Macbeth*. It was not a calculated decision. I had come that day from a village where about a dozen people had been murdered by the death squads, their thumbs tied behind their backs with wire and their throats slit.

I had read the play before, but in my other life as a student. A thirst for power at the cost of human life was no longer an abstraction to me. It was part of my universe.

I came upon Macduff's wife's speech made when the murderers, sent by Macbeth, arrive to kill her and her small children: "Whither should I fly?" she asks,

> I have done no harm. But I remember now
> I am in this earthly world—where to do harm
> Is often laudable, to do good sometime
> Accounted dangerous folly.[15]

Those words seized me like furies and cried out for the dead I had seen lined up that day in a dusty market square, the dead I have seen since, the dead, including the two thousand children who were killed in Sarajevo. The words cried out for those whom I would see later in unmarked mass graves in Bosnia, Kosovo, Iraq, the Sudan, Algeria, El Salvador, the dead who are my own, who carried notebooks, cameras, and a vanquished idealism and sad addiction into war and never returned. Of course resistance is usually folly, of course power exercised with ruthlessness will win, of course force easily snuffs out gentle people, the compassionate, and the decent. A repentant Lear, who was unable to love because of his thirst for power and self-adulation acknowledges this in the final moments of the play.

Shakespeare celebrates, at his best, this magnificence of failure. When we view our lives honestly from the inside we are all failures, all sinners, all in need of forgiveness. Shakespeare lays bare the myths that blind and deform our souls. He understands that the world of the flesh and the world of the spirit are indivisible, that they coexist in a paradox, ever present.

Shakespeare reminds us that though we may not do what we want, we are responsible for our lives. It does not matter what has been made of us; what matters is what we ourselves make of what has been done to us.

I returned from the Balkans to America in the fall of 1998, to a Nieman Fellowship at Harvard, after fifteen years abroad mostly reporting wars. I no longer had the emotional and physical resilience of youth. The curator of the Nieman program, Bill Kovach, suggested that I see James O. Freedman, the former president of Dartmouth, for advice on how to spend the year. Freedman recommended the classics and urged me to take Greek or Latin.

I had studied Greek in seminary so I opted for Latin. Of course, there is nothing sacred, or necessarily redeeming, about ancient texts. The German and Italian fascists used and misused classical literature, especially Virgil's *Aeneid*, in their propaganda. The Greeks and Romans embraced magic, slavery, the subjugation of women, racial triumphalism, animal sacrifice, and infanticide. The Roman emperors staged elaborate reenactments of battles in and outside the arena that saw hundreds and at times thousands of prisoners and slaves maimed and killed for sport. At lunchtime, in between shows, they publicly executed prisoners. Any democratic participation was the prerogative of male citizens and was snuffed out for long periods by tyrants and near-constant warfare.

But the classics offer a continuum with Western literature,

architecture, art, and political systems. Our country's past, our political and social philosophy, and our intellectual achievements and spiritual struggles cannot be connected without great holes in the fabric, and failures of understanding, if we are not conversant in the classics.

"All literature, all philosophical treatises, all the voices of antiquity," Cicero wrote, "are full of examples for imitation, which would all lie unseen in darkness without the light of literature."[16] Thucydides, knowing that Athens was doomed in the war with Sparta, consoled himself with the belief that his city's artistic and intellectual achievements would in the coming centuries overshadow raw Spartan militarism. Beauty and knowledge could, ultimately, triumph over power.

As my year at Harvard progressed, I devoured the classical authors but wasn't always as sure about taking on a dead language. One of my favorite professors, Kathleen Coleman, stopped me one morning and announced that I needed a purpose behind my slog through Latin. Once a week, she instructed, I would appear at her office prepared to do a translation of a poem by Catullus or passage from Virgil. I had never read Catullus, but came to love him.

Carrying my books, I retreated in the afternoons to the Smyth Classical Library within Widener Library, with its huge oak tables and sagging leather chairs. My fondest memories revolve around this sanctuary with its well-thumbed volumes, noisy heating system, and glass cases with dusty displays of items like Roman table legs. I was freed to step outside myself, to struggle with questions the cant of modern culture often allows us to ignore.

All idylls must end. Mine was shattered on March 24, 1999, when NATO began its bombing of Kosovo. I had come to

Cambridge from Kosovo. Kosovar Albanians I had known for three years were now missing or found dead along roadsides. I slept little. I was chained to the news reports. My translator in Kosova, Shukrije Gashi, a poet, vanished. (I returned to Kosovo that summer to find her family was searching for her in mass graves.) The horrors of Kosovo were abstractions to most people in Cambridge. I held a communion, in my final weeks at Harvard, with the long dead.

I had memorized a few poems by Catullus and parts of *The Aeneid*. I woke one morning well before dawn, haunted by a Catullus poem written to Calvus, whose lover Quintilia had died. Calvus had abandoned her, as I felt I had abandoned friends in Kosovo and an array of other conflicts. His grief was mingled with his guilt. In the end, these words give me a balm to my grief, a momentary solace, a little understanding:

If anything welcome or pleasing, Calvus, can be felt
by silent tombs in answer to our grief,
from that painful longing in which we renew old loves
and weep for friendships we once cast away,
Surely Quintilia does not lament her early death
as much as she rejoices in your love.[17]

To survive as a human being is possible only through love. And, when Thanatos is ascendant, the instinct must be to reach out to those we love, to see in them all the divinity, pity, and pathos of the human. And to recognize love in the lives of others—even those with whom we are in conflict—love that is like our own. It does not mean we will avoid war or death. It does not mean that we as distinct individuals will survive. But love, in its mystery, has its own power. It alone gives us meaning that endures. It alone allows us to embrace and cherish life. Love has power both to resist in our nature what we know we must resist, and to affirm what we know we must affirm. And love, as the poets remind us, is eternal.

NOTES

INTRODUCTION

1. Orwell, George, *1984* (San Diego: Harcourt Brace Jovanovich, 1949), p. 35.
2. Homer, *The Odyssey*, translated by Stanley Lombardo (Indianapolis: Hackett, 2000), p. 138.
3. Arendt, Hannah, *The Origins of Totalitarianism* (San Diego: Harcourt Brace Jovanovich, 1979), pp. 380–381.
4. García Márquez, Gabriel, *Chronicle of a Death Foretold* (New York: Knopf, 1983).

CHAPTER I
THE MYTH OF WAR

1. LeShan, Lawrence, *The Psychology of War* (New York: Helios, 1992), Chapter Two.
2. Weil, Simone, '*The Iliad*' or '*The Poem of Force*,' (Wallingford, PA: Pendle Hill Pamphlet, 1993), p. 11.
3. Shakespeare, William, *Troilus and Cressida*–"Dramatis Personae," (Boston: Riverside Shakespeare, Houghton Mifflin, 1974), p. 448.
4. Ibid., Act V, sc. ii, p. 486.
5. Caputo, Philip, *Rumor of War* (New York: Holt, Rinehart & Winston, 1977), p. 345.
6. Shakespeare, William, *Troilus and Cressida*, (Boston: Riverside Shakespeare, Houghton Mifflin, 1974), Act I, sc. i, p. 450.
7. Mowat, Farley, *And No Birds Sang* (Toronto: Seal, 1987), p. 195.

8. Shakespeare, William, *Troilus and Cressida*, (Boston: Riverside Shakespeare, Houghton Mifflin, 1974), Act V, sc. viii, p. 490.

9. Weil, Simone, *'The Iliad' or 'The Poem of Force'* (Wallingford, PA: Pendle Hill Pamphlet, 1993), p. 36.

10. *London Observer*, November 18, 1822, quoted in Samuel Hynes, *The Soldiers' Tale* (New York: Penguin, 1997), p. 17.

11. Myrivilis, Stratis, *Life in the Tomb* (London: Quartet Books, 1987), p. 137.

12. Freud, Sigmund, *Civilization and Its Discontents* (New York: W. W. Norton, 1989), p. 72.

13. Orwell, George, *Homage to Catalonia*, quoted by F. Dyson, *Weapons and Hope* (New York: Harper & Row, 1984), p. 129.

14. Lasch, Christopher, *The Culture of Narcissism* (New York: W. W. Norton, 1979), pp. 7, 15.

15. See Shakespeare's *Henry IV, Part One*, *Henry IV, Part Two*, and *Henry V.*

CHAPTER 2
THE PLAGUE OF NATIONALISM

1. Kiš, Danilo, *On Nationalism*, in the Appendix to Mark Thompson's *A Paper House* (London: Vintage,1992), p. 339.

2. Todorov, Tzvetan, *Facing the Extreme: Moral Life in the Concentration Camps* (New York: Metropolitan /Owl Books, 1996), p. 228.

3. Levi, Primo, *The Drowned and the Saved (I Sommersi e i Salvati)* (London: Abacus, 1991), quoted by Todorov, Tzvetan, *Facing the Extreme* (New York: Metropolitan/Owl Books, 1996), p. 238.

4. Duras, Marguerite, *The War: A Memoir* (New York: Pantheon, 1986), p. 48.

CHAPTER 3
THE DESTRUCTION OF CULTURE

1. Ignatieff, Michael, *The Warrior's Honor: Ethnic War and the Modern Conscience* (New York: Henry Holt, 1998), p. 56.

2. Shakespeare, William, *Othello* (Boston: The Riverside Shakespeare, Houghton Mifflin, 1974), Act IV, sc. i.

3. Sachs, Susan, *Newsday*, October 22, 1995, p. A04.

CHAPTER 4

THE SEDUCTION OF BATTLE AND THE PERVERSION OF WAR

1. Bartov, Omer, *Mirrors of Destruction* (New York: Oxford University Press, 2002), p. 45.

2. Remarque, Erich Maria, *All Quiet on the Western Front* (New York: Fawcett Crest, 1975), p. 114.

3. Browning, Christopher, *Ordinary Men: Reserve Police Battalion 101 and the Final Solution in Poland* (New York: HarperCollins, 1992), Ch. 18.

4. Ibid.

5. Ibid., p. 85.

6. Morante, Elsa, *History: A Novel (La Storia)*, (New York: Aventura/Vintage Books, 1984).

7. Auden, W. H., *Selected Poems* (London: Faber & Faber, 1981), p. 80.

8. Proust, Marcel, quoted in Alain De Botton, *How Proust Can Change Your Life* (London: Picador,1997), p. 197.

9. Bartov, *Mirrors of Destruction*, p. 189.

10. Ka'Tzetnik 135633, *House of Dolls* (London: Muller, Blond & White, 1986).

11. Bartov, *Mirrors of Destruction*, p. 193.

12. Ibid.

13. Gray, J. Glenn, *The Warriors* (Lincoln: University of Nebraska Press, 1998), pp. 61–62.

14. Kapuściński, Ryszard, *Another Day of Life* (London: Picador, 1988), p. 56.

15. Ibid.

16. Ibid., p. 57.

17. Arendt, Hannah, *The Origins of Totalitarianism* (New York: Harcourt Brace, 1979), Ch. 9.

18. Canetti, Elias, *Crowds and Power* (New York: Viking Press, 1962), p. 187.

19. Andrić, Ivo, *The Bridge on the Drina* (Chicago: University of Chicago Press, 1977), p. 15.
20. Gray, *The Warriors*, p. 90.
21. Ibid.
22. Levi, Primo, *Survival in Auschwitz (Se questo è un uomo)* (New York: Collier, 1961).

CHAPTER 5
THE HIJACKING AND RECOVERY OF MEMORY

1. Kundera, Milan, *The Book of Laughter and Forgetting* (New York: HarperPerennial, 1996), p. 4.
2. Dorfman, Ariel, *Widows* (New York: Aventura, 1983).
3. Feitlowitz, Marguerite, *The Lexicon of Terror* (New York: Oxford University Press, 1998).
4. Grossman, Vasily, *Life and Fate* (New York: Harper & Row, 1980), p. 82.

CHAPTER 6
THE CAUSE

1. Canetti, Elias, *Crowds and Power* (New York: Viking, 1962), p. 138.
2. Herr, Michael, *Dispatches* (New York: Vintage International, 1991), p. 215.
3. For an expansive portrait of Morel and the Congo, see Adam Hochschild, *King Leopold's Ghost* (Boston: Houghton Mifflin, 1998).
4. Arendt, Hannah, *The Origins of Totalitarianism*, discussed by Omer Bartov in his book, *Murder in Our Midst* (New York: Oxford University Press, 2000), p. 72.

CHAPTER 7
EROS AND THANATOS

1. Freud, Sigmund, *Civilization and Its Discontents* (New York: W. W. Norton, 1989), p. 82.
2. Loyd, Anthony, *My War Gone By, I Miss It So* (London: Doubleday, 1999), p. 136.
3. Grossman, Dave, *On Killing: The Psychological Cost of Learning to Kill in War and Society* (Boston: Little, Brown, 1996), pp. 43–44.
4. Gray, J. Glenn, *The Warriors* (Lincoln: University of Nebraska Press, 1998), p. 21.
5. *Ha'aretz*, English Edition, May 4, 2001, p. B3.
6. Sudetic, Chuck, *Blood and Vengeance* (New York: W. W. Norton, 1998), pp. xxxii–xxxiii.
7. Djilas, Milovan, *Wartime* (New York: Harvest Books, 1977), p. 280.
8. Fitzgerald, Robert, *In the Rose of Time: Poems 1931–1956* (New York: New Directions Books, 1956), p. 148.
9. Frankl, Viktor, *Man's Search for Meaning* (New York: Simon and Schuster, 1984), p. 48.
10. Vistica, Gregory L., "What happened in Thanh Phong," *The New York Times Magazine*, April 29, 2001, p. 51.
11. Farney, Dennis, *The Wall Street Journal*, April 25, 2001.
12. Manchester, William, *Goodbye Darkness: A Memoir of the Pacific War* (London: Dell, 1980), pp. 17–18.
13. Gray, *The Warriors*, p. 207.
14. Pyle, Ernie, *Ernies' War–the Best of Ernie Pyle's World War II Dispatches* (New York: Simon and Schuster, 1987), p. 419.
15. Shakespeare, William, *Macbeth* (Boston: Riverside Shakespeare, Houghton Mifflin, 1974), Act IV, sc. ii.
16. Cicero, *Pro Archia*, 2.3. 14–16, quoted in Bernard Knox, *The Oldest Dead White European Males* (New York: W. W. Norton, 1993), p. 83.
17. Goold, George, *Catullus* (London: Duckworth, 1983).

BIBLIOGRAPHY

Andrić, Ivo. *The Bridge on the Drina*. Chicago: University of Chicago Press, 1977.

————. *Conversations with Goya: Bridges, Signs* London: Menard Press, 1992.

Armstrong, Karen. *The Battle for God*. New York: Knopf, 2000.

Arendt, Hannah. *The Origins of Totalitarianism*. New York: Harcourt Brace, 1976.

Auden, W. H. *Selected Poems*. Boston: Faber & Faber, 1979.

Bartov, Omer. *Mirrors of Destruction*. New York: Oxford University Press, 1996.

————. *Murder in our Midst*. New York: Oxford University Press, 2000.

Blunden, Edmund. *Undertones of War*. London: Penguin, 1984.

Browning, Christopher. *Ordinary Men*. New York: HarperCollins, 1992.

Canetti, Elias. *Crowds and Power*. New York: Viking, 1962.

Caputo, Philip. *A Rumor of War*. New York: Holt, Rinehart and Winston, 1977.

Carroll, Lewis. *Alice's Adventures in Wonderland*. New York: Oxford University Press, 1971.

Céline, Louis-Ferdinand. *Castle to Castle (D'un Chateau l'Autre)*. New York: Carroll & Graf, 1988.

————. *Journey to the End of the Night* (Voyage au Bout de la Nuit) New York: New Directions, 1983.

Conrad, Joseph. *Heart of Darkness*. New York: Knopf, 1993.

————. *Lord Jim*. Evanston, Illinois: Harper & Row, 1963.

————. *Victory*. New York: Doubleday, 1957.

De Botton, Alain. *How Proust Can Change Your Life*. London: Picador, 1997.

Djilas, Milovan. *Wartime*. New York: Harcourt Brace Jovanovich, 1977.

Dorfman, Ariel. *Widows*. New York: Aventura, 1984.

Duras, Marguerite. *The War: a Memoir.* New York: Pantheon, 1986.

Eliot, T. S. *What Is a Classic?* New York: Faber & Faber, 1950.

Feitlowitz, Margarite. *A Lexicon of Terror: Argentina and the Legacies of Torture.* New York: Oxford University Press, 1998.

Ferguson, Niall. *The Pity of War.* London: Allen Lane, 1998.

Fitzgerald, Robert. *In the Rose of Time; Poems 1931–1956.* Norfolk, Conn.: James Laughlin, 1956.

Forster, E. M. *Two Cheers for Democracy.* New York: Harcourt Brace, 1951.

Frankl, Victor. *Man's Search for Meaning.* New York: Simon and Schuster, 1984.

Freud, Sigmund. *Civilization and Its Discontents.* New York: W. W. Norton, 1989.

———. *On Creativity and the Unconscious.* New York: Harper & Row, 1958.

Fussell, Paul. *The Great War and Modern Memory.* Oxford, England: Oxford University Press, 1977.

García Márquez, Gabriel. *Chronicle of a Death Foretold.* New York: Knopf, 1983.

Graves, Robert. *Goodbye to All That.* Middlesex, England: Penguin, 1986.

———. *The Greek Myths I and II.* London: Penguin, 1960.

Gray, J. Glenn. *The Warriors.* Lincoln: University of Nebraska Press, 1998.

Grossman, David. *On Killing: The Psychological Cost of Learning to Kill in War and Society.* Boston: Little, Brown, 1996.

Grossman, Vasily. *Life and Fate.* New York: Harper & Row, 1980.

Halbwachs, Maurice. *La Mémoire Collective.* Paris: Albin Michel, 1950.

Herr, Michael. *Dispatches.* New York: Vintage International, 1991.

Hochschild, Adam. *King Leopold's Ghost.* Boston: Houghton Mifflin, 1998.

Hollander, Paul. *Political Pilgrims.* New York: Harper Colophon, 1981.

Holmes, Richard. *Firing Line.* London: Pimlico, 1994.

Homer, translated by Stanley Lombardo. *The Iliad.* Indianapolis: Hackett, 1997.

———. *Odyssey.* Indianapolis: Hackett, 2000.

Hume, David. *A Treatise on Human Nature.* Oxford, England: Clarendon Press, 1968.

Hynes, Samuel. *The Soldiers' Tale.* New York: Penguin, 1997.

Ignatieff, Michael. *The Warrior's Honor.* New York: Henry Holt, 1997.

Jones, James. *From Here to Eternity.* Glasgow: Collins, 1987.

Junger, Ernst. *Storm of Steel: From the Diary of a German Storm-troop Officer on the Western Front.* New York: Fertig, 1996.

Kapuściński, Ryszard. *Another Day of Life.* London: Picador, 1988.

Ka"Tzetnik 135633. *House of Dolls.* London: Miller, Blond, & White, 1986.

Keegan, John. *The Face of Battle.* London: Jonathan Cape Ltd., 1976.

———. *A History of Warfare.* London: Random House, 1994.

Knightley, Phillip. *The First Casualty.* New York: Harcourt Brace Jovanovich, 1975.

Knox, Bernard. *The Oldest Dead White European Males.* New York: W. W. Norton, 1993.

Koestler, Arthur. *Scum of the Earth.* London: Eland, 1991.

Kundera, Milan. *The Book of Laughter and Forgetting.* New York: Harper Perennial, 1996.

Larkin, Philip. *Collected Poems.* New York: Farrar, Straus and Giroux, 1989.

———. *Required Writing.* Boston: Faber & Faber, 1986.

Lasch, Christopher. *The Culture of Narcissism.* New York: W. W. Norton, 1979.

LeShan, Lawrence. *The Psychology of War.* New York: Helios, 1992.

Levi, Primo. *The Drowned and the Saved (I Sommersi e i Salvati).* London: Abacus, 1991.

———. *Survival in Auschwitz (Se questo è un uomo).* New York: Collier, 1987.

Loyd, Anthony. *My War Gone By, I Miss It So.* London: Doubleday, 1999.

Mailer, Norman. *The Naked and the Dead.* London: Panther, 1984.

Manchester, William. *Goodbye Darkness: A Memoir of the Pacific War.* New York: Dell, 1980.

Manning, Frederic. *The Middle Parts of Fortune.* London: Penguin, 2000.

Marshall, S. L. A. *Men Against Fire.* Norman: University of Oklahoma Press, 2000.

Melville, Herman. *Moby-Dick.* New York: W. W. Norton, 1967.

Morante, Elsa. *History: A Novel (La Storia).* New York: Aventura, 1984.

Myrivilis, Stratis. *Life In the Tomb.* London: Quartet, 1987.

Niebuhr, Reinhold. *The Children of Life and The Children of Darkness.* New York: Charles Scribner's Sons, 1972.

———. *Moral Man and Immoral Society*. New York: Charles Scribner's Sons, 1960.

———. *The Nature and Destiny of Man Vol. I and II*. New York: Charles Scribner's Sons, 1964.

Orwell, George. *Homage to Catalonia*. New York: Harcourt Brace Jovanovich, 1952.

———. *1984*. New York: Harcourt Brace Jovanovich, 1977.

Owen, Wilfred. *Selected Poems*. London: Bloomsbury, 1995.

Pyle, Ernie. *Ernie's War*. New York: Simon and Schuster, 1986.

Remarque, Erich Maria. *All Quiet on the Western Front*. New York: Fawcett Crest, 1958.

Roth, Joseph. *Hotel Savoy*. Woodstock, N.Y.: Overlook Press, 1986.

———. *The Radetzky March*. London: Penguin, 1974.

Shakespeare, William. *The Riverside Shakespeare*, edited by G. Blakemore Evans. Boston: Houghton Mifflin, 1974.

Silkin, Jon (ed.). *The Penguin Book of First World War Poetry*. London: Penguin, 1996.

Sudetic, Chuck. *Blood and Vengeance*. New York: W. W. Norton, 1998.

Thompson, Mark. *A Paper House*. London: Vintage, 1992.

Thucydides. *A Comprehensive Guide to The Peloponnesian War*, edited by Robert B. Strassler. New York: Touchstone, 1998.

Todorov, Tzvetan. *Facing the Extreme: Moral Life in the Concentration Camps*. New York: Metropolitan/Owl Books, 1996.

Wiesel, Elie. *Night*. New York: Avon, 1960.

Zimmerman, Warren. *Origins of a Catastrophe*. New York: Times Books, 1996.

ACKNOWLEDGMENTS

IT HAS BEEN NEARLY TWENTY YEARS SINCE I GRADUATED from Harvard Divinity School and left Cambridge to cover the war in El Salvador. This book is not only the result of my work in various war zones, but is a product of the education I received, especially in English literature and Christian theology, at Colgate University and Harvard University. I owe much of what I am to great professors—Coleman Brown, Margaret Maurer, Krister Stendhal, G. Blakemore Evans, W. Jackson Bate, Robert Coles, and Robert Pinsky. They taught me how to read and write and most importantly how to think critically. I have carried their wisdom, their love of books, and their moral probity with me. I have tried to live a life by the standards they set.

Peter Osnos, the publisher of PublicAffairs, conceived of the book idea and pushed me to make it work. He then went on to publish it. He turned me over to his executive editor, Paul Golob, whose talent and good humor carried me through. It is a much better book for Paul's willingness to read and reread with such care and intelligence. David Patterson at PublicAffairs ironed out all the kinks and made the logistics work. Lisa Bankoff of International Creative Management shepherded me through the world of book publishing with grace and wisdom.

My editors at *The New York Times*, Jon Landman, Ann Cronin, Christine Kay, and Bill Goss are not only immensely talented but blessed with infinite patience. Moreover, they stand up for the reporters who work for them. I want to thank colleagues and editors at *The New York Times* over the years, including Bernie Gwertzman, whose decency and equanimity made him truly loved, Andy Rosenthal, Bill Keller, Chris Wren, Ethan Bronner, Eric Eckholm, Helen Verongos, Marie Courtney, Cynthia Latimer-Ortiz, Kathy Rose, Steve Weisman, Tom Feyer, Eric Schmitt, Steve Kinzer, Jeanne Moore, Ed Marks, Chris Drew, and Susan Sachs. The editors at *Harper's* magazine, in particular John R. MacArthur, Lewis H. Lapham, and Ben Metcalf, keep alive the marriage between great writing and great thought and somehow make my pieces sing. I would also like to thank the editors I work with at *Foreign Affairs*, especially James F. Hoge Jr. and Celia Whitaker, along with Fareed Zakaria, now with *Newsweek*. Also, my colleagues at New York University, especially William and Judy Serrin, Carol Sternhell, Michael and Beth Norman and Cathleen Dullahan, all keep alive great journalism traditions. Eva Sanchez, Puja Vaswani, and Caroline Bingham worked tirelessly as researchers. They, and the staff at the New York University library, were vital. My NYU library privileges are among my most precious possessions.

Coleman Brown, Peter Meineck, Kim Parham, Jack Wheeler, who lent his considerable intellect as well as his experience as a professional soldier, Linda McNell, and Claudia Wassmann worked on the manuscript and made many important changes and corrections. They gave it greater clarity and depth. I owe a huge debt to the colleagues I worked with over the years—especially Lajla Veselica and Wade Goddard in Croatia and Ivana Sekularac in Serbia; these three kept me balanced and were able, when I most needed it, to make me laugh at myself. Boba Lizdek in Sarajevo and now Paris, Shukrije Gashi, my translator in Kosovo who was later killed by the Serbs, Alija Dedajić, whose wits saved both our lives during the war in Bosnia more than once, Jadranka Milanović, the late Miladin Zivotić, and Serif Turgut were priceless companions. Tom Gjelten and Neil Conan at National Public Radio, Kanan Makiya, Tony Horwitz and Geraldine Brooks, Jim Landers, Michael Ignatieff, Iliriana Bajo, Ivo Banac, Malika Berak—who introduced me to two of my favorite writers, Marcel Proust and Louis-Ferdinand Céline—Rina Castelnouvo, Omar Othman, Gamal Mohei al-Din, Michael Georgy, Carlos Ramos, Emma Daley, Chuck Sudetic, Max Marcus, Kit Roane, Hani Sabra, Edward Said, and Alan Chin all contributed to my understanding and became close friends. Kurt Schork and Miguel Gil Morano, two brave and fine war correspondents, who were killed in May 2000 in an ambush in Sierra Leone, will remain with me always. I want to also thank Michael and Yora Kisch, Douglas and Ellen Davidson, Robert Kaplan, Sören and Charlotte Liborius, Alina Margolis, Daniel Reed, Walter and Ann Pincus, Ward Pincus and Iobel Andemicael, Christine Hauser, Ravi Sidhu, David and Yael Amir, Patricia Diermeier, Elise Colette, and the great and very funny political cartoonist Joe Sacco.

I spent the academic year 1998–1999 at Harvard as a Nieman Fellow thanks to generosity of Joe Lelyveld and *The New York Times*. During the year I developed a close friendship with the curator, Bill Kovach, an inspirational man and one of the finest journalists I have ever known. Bill, along with Julie Felt, Chris Marquis, Mary and Lawrence Walsh, Kathy Coleman, Richard Thomas, Frank and Margo Lindsey,

Zeph Stewart, James and Sheba Freedman, Lily Galily, and Susan Reed, made that year one of the richest of my life.

I owe more than I can repay to Josyane Séchaud, who endured the long absences, the danger, and frequent uncertainty from El Salvador to Kosovo, with Swiss stoicism and unwavering understanding and support. My mother, Teddy Hedges, a professor of English, imparted to me a love of books and writing. She was the first one to publish my work, in a booklet she typed and bound when I was a child. My aunt and uncle, Miriam and Ellsworth Blair, make our retreats to Maine possible and somehow put up with my wildnesss. But my greatest thanks go to Thomas and Nöelle, who remind me every day that my chief role, and the one I value most, is as a father. I hope they never do what I did.

INDEX

PUBLICAFFAIRS is a publishing house founded in 1997. It is a tribute to the standards, values, and flair of three persons who have served as mentors to countless reporters, writers, editors, and book people of all kinds, including me.

I. F. STONE, proprietor of *I. F. Stone's Weekly,* combined a commitment to the First Amendment with entrepreneurial zeal and reporting skill and became one of the great independent journalists in American history. At the age of eighty, Izzy published *The Trial of Socrates,* which was a national bestseller. He wrote the book after he taught himself ancient Greek.

BENJAMIN C. BRADLEE was for nearly thirty years the charismatic editorial leader of *The Washington Post.* It was Ben who gave the *Post* the range and courage to pursue such historic issues as Watergate. He supported his reporters with a tenacity that made them fearless, and it is no accident that so many became authors of influential, best-selling books.

ROBERT L. BERNSTEIN, the chief executive of Random House for more than a quarter century, guided one of the nation's premier publishing houses. Bob was personally responsible for many books of political dissent and argument that challenged tyranny around the globe. He is also the founder and was the longtime chair of Human Rights Watch, one of the most respected human rights organizations in the world.

.   .   .

For fifty years, the banner of Public Affairs Press was carried by its owner Morris B. Schnapper, who published Gandhi, Nasser, Toynbee, Truman, and about 1,500 other authors. In 1983 Schnapper was described by *The Washington Post* as "a redoubtable gadfly." His legacy will endure in the books to come.

Peter Osnos, *Publisher*

The Search for a Common Narrative
. the most precious & elusive
of all narratives — truth. pp 81-82.